THE SURFING HANDBOOK

MASTERING THE WAVES
for Beginning and Amateur Surfers

+ TIPS from the PROS!

BY BEN MARCUS
Photographs by Kara Kanter

MVP
BOOKS

Acknowledgments:

My thanks to Jefferson "Zuma Jay" Wagner, Carla Rowland, Cory Bluemling, Rochelle Ballard, Lucia Griggi, Brie Gabrielle, Joe Dalsanto, and Patricia Dwyer, who authored the "Wetsuit Styles" section and the "Wetsuit Glossary" sidebar. And of course to King Neptune for providing the waves.

First published in 2010 by MVP Books, an imprint of MBI Publishing Company, 400 First Avenue North, Suite 300, Minneapolis, MN 55401 USA

MVP Books titles are also available at discounts in bulk quantity for industrial or sales-promotional use. For details write to Special Sales Manager at MBI Publishing Company, 400 First Avenue North, Suite 300, Minneapolis, MN 55401 USA.

To find out more about our books, visit us online at www.voyageurpress.com.

ISBN-13: 978-0-7603-3692-2

Library of Congress Cataloging-in-Publication Data

Marcus, Ben, 1960-
  The surfing handbook : mastering the waves for beginning and amateur surfers / by Ben Marcus ; photographs by Kara Kanter.
       p. cm.
    Includes index.
    ISBN 978-0-7603-3692-2 (sb : alk. paper)
  1. Surfing--Handbooks, manuals, etc. I. Title.
  GV839.5.M38 2010
  797.3'2--dc22
                                          2009045901

Editor: Michael Dregni

Design Manager: Katie Sonmor

Layout by: Erin Fahringer

Designed by: Sandra Salimony

Table of Contents

chapter 1

Why We Surf: A Magnificent Obsession

REMEMBER THE 1991 HOLLYWOOD FILM *POINT BREAK*, when Keanu Reeves goes into the oceanside surf shop to buy a beginner surfboard and meets the surfer grommet running the store? The kid is maybe 13, his skin tanned to a golden hue, his hair bleached blond by the sun.

Below left: Waves have as many moods and personalities as people, and one of the adventures of surfing is getting to know them all. *Epic Stock/Shutterstock. Center:* The author as a young grommet with his first surfboard, circa 1973. *Photo by Mom. Right:* A Hawaiian *lei* awaits on the shore. *Bonita R. Cheshier*

Hawaiian surfriders as depicted in 1878 by missionary Reverend J. G. Wood in his exposé of *The Uncivilized Races of Man in All Countries of the World*. Even way back then, those waveriders looked happy.

And he's handing out life advice. Reeves plays an FBI special agent named Johnny Utah who wants to learn to surf as a cover to infiltrate a suspected gang of surfing bank robbers. The surf shop grom tells him, "Surfing's the source, man. It will change your life—swear to God."

That scene might have been a tad bit corny, but the grommet had a point. Surfing is a journey of a thousand adventures that begins with a single step into the ocean.

I began surfing when I was that grommet's age, about 13, in 1973. I grew up in Santa Cruz, California—one of the surfing world's several ground zeroes. My first surfboard was made in the 1970s by shaper Doug Haut at a time when surfboards were undergoing a transition from longboards to short. There was a lot of

Talk The Talk

A **grommet** is a young surfer. "Grommet" is not generally a slam; the term is often used about hot young surfers. The shortened version is **grom** or **grem**, which derives from **gremlin**.

A **surfboard shaper** is a surfboard maker who planes and sands a board to the desired shape—a job requiring incredible skill, experience, and patience.

experimentation at the time, which lead to some weird boards. My first board, in retrospect, was a little weird.

But I loved that surfboard, and I carried it to the beach, almost every day, walking from Seventh Avenue to Cowell's Beach, a distance of some 2½ miles (4 kilometers). I strolled with my board along the Santa Cruz Beach Boardwalk, down onto the sand, under the pier, and then out into the Pacific Ocean, where I spent hour after hour, learning how to surf at one of the best beginner spots in California—and the world.

I was a bit of a lost boy then, the child of a divorce that came when I was just entering my teens and needing the guidance that all kids that age need. After the divorce, it was cool that we had moved from the Santa Clara Valley to Santa Cruz, and learning to surf was fun and

Left: Surfing, then. Synchronized swimming starlet Esther Williams styles as a surfer girl, circa 1940s. *Below:* Surfing, now. If it's a life of adventure you want, surfing will give you a lifetime of adventure. You can surf it all, but you will never have surfed it all. *Lucia Griggi*

Others surf because they fall in love with the ocean and with how paddling makes your back and arm muscles feel. Surfing has a lot to love, from sunrise to sunset. *Michelle Geft*

exciting and challenging. But the children of divorce are always a little shook up and lonely. I have since seen a pattern in a lot of surfers—including a lot of *great* surfers, from Miki Dora to Kelly Slater—who turned to the ocean after their families fell apart.

That's probably what I was doing, because I have since learned that if you spend several hours a day in the ocean, paddling in cold water, the endorphins and adrenaline and other "liqueurs of fear" are so overwhelming that it's impossible to be depressed, to feel bad.

So I surfed, a lot, every day I could, doing that long walk, 5 miles (8 kilometers) a day carrying a heavy surfboard and wearing a quarter-inch diving wetsuit that I bought from O'Neill's Dive Shop (because I didn't know any better). Surfing felt good. I lost weight. I ate well. If I was depressed from the broken home, the endorphins and adrenaline

Surfing's an unusual thing to do, really: to sit on a piece of plastic out to sea, with lots of sky and clouds above, and the mysterious ocean below, using your knowledge and your strength and your skill to hunt down and ride bands of energy sent from thousands of miles away. *Shutterstock*

kept all that bad feeling at bay. All the exercise and exertion let me sleep like a baby. Or so I thought. My mom tells a story of me walking through the kitchen, which was between my bedroom and the bathroom. I had a pillow under my arm where that purple Haut surfboard usually was.

Mom looked at me and said, "Ben, are you okay?"

I responded, or so she says, "Yeah, but I can't find any waves."

And I went back to bed. Sleepwalking. Stoked to be a surfer.

Amazingly, impossibly, those were some of the best times of my life: Walking miles to the beach carrying a weird surfboard, wearing the wrong wetsuit, paddling out at Cowell's, learning the secrets of the sea, learning to surf.

Learning to surf is one of the hardest things you will ever do. But if you learn, and you keep going with it, and you do it every day or as often as possible, the initial investment of time, money, struggle, embarrassment, and sunburn will pay off in a lifetime of good feeling, better health, adventures you never thought possible, friendships, stories, and a good tan.

You've read the slogans on a thousand bumper stickers:

"Only a surfer knows the feeling."

"Surfing is better than sex."

"Surfing is my addiction."

"Work is for those who don't surf."

"If you don't surf, don't start. If you do surf, never stop."

You've read the slogans, but the truth is this: They're all true—from the muscles in your back to the happy chemicals in your head; eating better, sleeping better, feeling better. Life's just better when you add surfing to it.

But I repeat: Learning to surf is not easy. The equipment is confusing, the ocean is scary, and even experienced athletes must learn to use new muscles, new balance points, new skills. Learning to surf is complicated, but having an experienced hand to guide you can make the experience a whole lot easier. There are many things to consider: Which surfboard is the right length for you with the right amount of flotation? What wetsuit and booties and rash guard should you wear? Which side of the board does the wax go on? How do you paddle so you aren't too far forward or too far back? How do you paddle out through the surfline and find the right place to catch the wave? How do you make it from prone to knees to standing? And what do you do after that?

Learning to surf is a matter of knowing yourself, learning the secrets of the sea, and making the two come together. Going out and doing all this on your own is one way to do it, but one of the big barriers in

Opposite Page: Others say surfing is like a drug. And it's true that it makes food taste better, makes hot showers feel better, and helps you sleep like a baby. *Richard Clarke/Shutterstock*

learning to surf isn't mental or physical. It's temporal—time. It takes time to learn how to surf, and one way to condense the learning curve is to take the hand of an experienced instructor who will put you on the right board in the right spot and get you up and riding—get you started on the right foot, whether it's goofy or regular.

Others do it for the love, because they fall in love with the ocean and with how paddling makes your back and arm muscles feel. Surfing has a lot to love, from sunrise to sunset, and even surfing under the full moon, in a red tide, watching the phosphorescence swirling under your hands and between your fingertips.

Talk the Talk

A **regular foot** is a surfer who rides with their left leg forward.

A **goofy foot** surfs with their right leg forward.

It's an unusual thing to do, really: to sit on a piece of plastic out to sea, with lots of sky and clouds above and the mysterious ocean below, using your knowledge and your strength and your skill to hunt down and ride bands of energy sent from thousands of miles away, open ocean swells generated by storms of unimaginable power, which send scrambled potency fanning out into the ocean. That force organizes itself and travels for hundreds and thousands of miles, then approaches beaches, points, rivermouths, jetties and other obstructions, and is shaped into waves.

Waves have as many moods and personalities as people, and one of the adventures of surfing is getting to know all of them. Start at your local beach, struggling with yourself and equipment and learning your steps. As you get better, you get your beginner break figured out, then move up into a whole big world of new kinds of waves, new experiences: long, perfect green walls breaking for a quarter mile (400 meters) on the Australian point breaks, exotic reef breaks in the Mentawai islands of Indonesia, the beachbreaks of France when the offshore winds carry the scent of grapes and wine casks.

If it's a life of adventure you want, surfing will give you a lifetime of adventure. You can surf it all, but you will never have surfed it all.

If it's a life of good health you want, surfing will give that to you too. If you start surfing and you never stop, you will have a stronger back, stronger arms, better skin (if you wear sunscreen), and a strong stomach from all that paddling. If they could bottle and sell the health benefits of surfing, someone would make a fortune.

And surfing is as good for you internally and externally. Want to be good and hungry? Go surf 8-foot (2.4-meter) waves in 54-degree water for six hours, paddling hard the whole way. And then see how hungry you are. Eat as much as you want, because when you are surfing hard, your body needs every extra calorie, leaving nothing extra on you at all.

They say that surfing is like a drug. And it's true that it makes food taste better, makes hot showers feel better, helps you sleep like a baby—all the positive effects of narcotics and drugs, but with none of the downside, with the exception of the occasional embarrassing sinus drain as your nose empties out trapped ocean water in an uncontrollable gush.

An amped little grommet catches a wave and shows how it's done. His smile is almost as wide as the ocean.
Lucia Griggi

A surfer cuts across the top of a wave, sending spray skyward. *Epic Stock/Shutterstock*

Now think back to the end of *Point Break*. Johnny Utah has tracked the bad guy, Bodhi (played by Patrick Swayze) around the world to the famed Bell's Beach, Victoria, Australia, where Bodhi is going to ride the monster waves created by a 50-year storm. These two guys have tried to kill each other several times. They're enemies, but what is the first thing they say to each other?

"Still surfing?" Bodhi asks.

To which Johnny Utah responds, "Every day."

And that part is true, too. Once you start surfing, and it really puts its hooks into you—that's how it makes you behave.

Surfing *is* the source. It *will* change your life. Swear to God.

This book takes in my own experience and the experience of a whole lot of better surfers to help you take those first steps.

chapter 2

Selecting a Surfboard

THE NUMBER-ONE MISTAKE most beginners make is to try to surf on a board that is too short, too thin, and too narrow. The bigger and thicker and wider the surfboard, the more flotation it will have, and flotation is like training wheels for a beginner surfer. The formula is simple:

More speed + more stability = an easier platform for catching and riding waves

Left: The number-one mistake most beginners make is to try to surf on a board that is too short, too thin, and too narrow. The bigger and thicker and wider the surfboard, the more flotation it will have. *Epic Stock/Shutterstock. Right:* The array of different surfboards—and even surfboard fins—can be daunting to novices. *Lucia Griggi*

Left: Jefferson "Zuma Jay" Wagner is so busy, he doesn't have time for a costume change between the time he closes his surf shop and gets a wave in, to when he has to be at his "other" job as a Malibu city councilman. So, to save time, he wears a drip-dry suit. Not. *Lucia Griggi*

Below: Shortboards behind him, longboards above, Zuma Jay walks novice surfers through the many different styles of surfboards, explaining what is right for beginners. Zuma Jay stocks all kinds of surfboards, from 5-foot (1½-meter) Fish to 12-foot (3¾-meter) SUP. There are many to choose from, but choosing wisely can be the different between failing and standing.

Beginning surfers are going to be as awkward in the water as baby ducks are on land. Riding the wrong equipment makes the whole process more difficult—and sometimes impossible. The local surfers at Malibu or Australian breaks see this all the time: beginners flopping and flailing around on the wrong surfboards. Often these are boards that even an experienced surfer would have trouble riding.

Zuma Jay's Surf Shop, just south of the Malibu Pier, on the Pacific Coast Highway in California has new surfers walking in the front door every day looking for a first surfboard. Zuma Jay, also known as Jefferson Wagner, has been the owner since 1975, when the shop first opened on California's Zuma Beach. For 35 years now, he has helped generations of beginning surfers choose that first board.

Most novices walk into Zuma Jay's shop with wide eyes like kids in a candy store, checking out all the exotic board shapes and lengths and colors. There are a lot of boards to buy that are sleek and chic and cool and endorsed by the coolest surfers on the planet. That is nice for window-shopping and future dreams, but the best move for a beginner

continued on page 25

Surfboards in All Shapes and Sizes

THE SURFBOARD has been evolving for hundreds of years, from the willi willi and redwood *olo* and *alaia* of the Polynesians to the modern world's balsa wood, fiberglass, and resin and the more exotic materials and construction techniques of the twenty-first century. Never has there been a greater variety of surfboard styles, made in a wider variety of materials, than now. It may be confusing to the beginner, so hopefully this quick history of surfboard types will help.

BODYBOARD
Early on, the Polynesians rode waves laying prone on *paipo* boards. But that style of wave riding was overtaken by surfboard riding—until the 1970s, that is, when Malibu surfer Tom Morey developed the **Morey Boogie**, a 4-foot-6-inch-long by 23-inch-wide (1.4-meter-long by 58-centimeter-wide) bellyboard made out of closed-cell polyethylene foam. Morey started a new craze that has seen bodyboarding outsell surfing four to one in the total number of boards sold. Bodyboards are well-suited for some kinds of waves, but are not allowed in other places—such as Malibu itself, where bodyboarders are forbidden from riding waves along the entire point.

In the early years of surfing, monstrous boards such as this 1930s Pacific Home Systems Swastika redwood board got many a Waikiki tourist hooked on waveriding.

ALAIA

A traditional Hawaiian surfboard going back to the eighteenth and nineteenth centuries that has become popular among some surfers in the twenty-first century. In old Hawaii, the *ali'i* (royalty) rode the longer *olo* surfboards while the commoners rode shorter, finless shaped pieces of wood called *alaia*. The modern *alaia* are anywhere from 5 feet 5 inches (1.7 meters) to 10 feet (3 meters) long, a half to an inch (1.3 to 2.5 centimeters) thick, and 15 to 18 inches (38 to 46 centimeters) wide. Riding waves on a piece of wood with no fin is extremely difficult. Modern *alaia* surfers slide the tail to control direction and speed.

Alaia boards were surfed by Hawaiians well into the twentieth century. This *koa* 7-foot 9-inch (2.5-meter) replica was shaped by master surfer and boardbuilder Greg Noll in 1998. *Fernando Aguerre collection/Juliana Morais*

OLO

The *olo* were hardwood boards as long as 16 feet (4.9 meters) that were ridden exclusively by the Polynesian royalty. The penalty for a commoner caught riding one of these boards was death. The Hawaiian monarchy was usurped in the 1880s by American interests, and the sport of surfing faded, as did the use of the *olo*. In the 1920s, a Wisconsin native named Tom Blake rediscovered the *olo* at Hawaii's Bishop Museum and began making modern versions of the ancient boards. The *olo* paddled better and could catch more waves than the *alaia*, and the modern surfboard evolved from Tom Blake's surf archaeology.

This 12-foot 6-inch (3.75-meter) solid *koa* wood *olo* was shaped by Greg Noll as a tribute to the ancient Hawaiians. Only royalty were allowed to surf *olos*, and thus they were rare and special boards. *Fernando Aguerre collection/Juliana Morais*

LONGBOARD

All surfboards were "longboards" until the shortboard revolution of the late 1960s. Longboarding began to fade away in the late 1960s, but was brought back in the late 1970s. In modern times, a longboard is a board 8 or 9 feet (2 or 3 meters) or longer with a rounded nose. Longboards are longer, wider, and thicker than the typical shortboard, all of which makes them easier to paddle and catch waves. Longboard surfing differs from shortboard surfing in that longboarders move from the tail to the tip of the nose and back to negotiate waves.

A classic Duke Kahanamoku longboard from 1965, measuring 9 feet 6 inches (3 meters). *Fernando Aguerre collection/Juliana Morais*

Surfing's first hero, Hawaiian waterman Duke Paoa Kahanamoku, stands proud beneath a towering *olo* on Waikiki Beach.

MALIBU OR MINI-MAL

In the mid-1950s, a group of southern California surfers brought their lightweight balsa wood Malibu Chip surfboards to Australia, and longboards have been called "Malibu" in Australia ever since. To some, Malibu is synonymous with longboard. To others, a Malibu is a longboard shape that is shorter than a typical longboard and has a slimmer outline and a thinner tail for performance surfing. Some people see a Malibu—or a shorter **mini-Mal**—as the same as a **funboard** (see page 20). Malibus typically have one or three fins.

This 1950s Malibu was made of solid balsa wood and measured 7 feet 7 inches (2.25 meters). *Fernando Aguerre collection/Juliana Morais*

POPOUT

A derisive term for quickly made and inexpensively produced boards. A variety of techniques exist, but generally popouts are molded boards that are not hand-shaped and fiberglassed. The popout arrived in 1959, and the boards were considered inferior and cheap through most of the twentieth century; real surfers rode custom-made boards. At the turn of the century, Santa Cruz shaper Randy French converted sailboard-manufacturing techniques to surfboards and began producing **Surftech** boards, which while still technically popouts, are also stronger and lighter than conventional boards and made in a wide variety of shapes, styles, colors, and flavors.

HYBRID

Some say shortboards are no longer than 7 feet (2 meters); some say longboards don't start until 9 feet (2.7 meters). In between is the hybrid—an intermediate board for intermediate surfers. Hybrids are popular with experienced surfers getting too old or large for a shortboard, but also with beginners making a transition from longboards to shortboards. The typical hybrid is 8 feet (2.4 meters) long and as wide as 22 inches (56 centimeters), with a nose wide like a longboard but a tail narrow like a shortboard. Hybrids float better and are more stable than shortboards, but aren't as big and cumbersome as shortboards. Some consider mini-Mals, funboards, and hybrids as all the same thing, although a hybrid is generally considered a performance surfboard.

GUN

In 1964, surfer Buzzy Trent was one of the best big-wave riders in the world. He was also a board shaper. While making a 12-foot (3.7-meter) big-wave board for Malibu surfer Joe Quigg, he announced, "You don't go hunting elephants with a BB gun. If you're going to hunt big waves, take a big gun." Ever since, surfboards designed for riding big or extreme waves are called "guns." Big-wave guns are 7 feet (2 meters) or longer and shaped like shortboards, with enough flotation to allow surfers to paddle into big waves, but with pointed noses and narrow tails and outlines allowing for the speed and performance surfers need to make big waves. Guns from 7 to 9 feet (2 to 3 meters) meant for riding intense waves like Pipeline and (small) Teahupoo are sometimes called **mini guns**.

A 1954 balsa wood gun measuring 9 feet (2.75 meters). *Fernando Aguerre collection/Juliana Morais*

STANDUP PADDLEBOARD

A standup paddleboard, also known as an SUP is a surfboard as long as 18 feet (5.5 meters), as wide as 34 inches (86 centimeters), and as thick as 5 inches (12.7 centimeters), providing a stable platform for surfers standing up and propelling themselves across the water and/or into waves using a paddle. This style of surfing goes back to the Waikiki Beach Boys at the turn of the nineteenth into the twentieth centuries. It was popularized by Laird Hamilton, Brian Keaulana, and others at the turn of the 20th and 21st centuries. SUP surfers have an advantage over traditional surfers, as their height above the water allows them to see incoming waves, and the boards catch waves as if they were flicked along by the invisible hand of King Neptune.

THRUSTER

A three-fin surfboard innovated and popularized by Australian surfer/shaper Simon Anderson in 1981. The Thruster has a large central fin and two smaller side fins to provide thrust, hence the name. Since 1981, a majority of all surfboards shaped, sold, and ridden are Thrusters. Anderson did not patent his design, something he most likely regrets.

SHORTBOARD

In 1967, the World Contest at Ocean Beach, San Diego, came down to Australian Nat Young surfing from the tail on a thin 9-foot 4-inch (2.8-meter) board he called Magic Sam, versus David Nuuhiwa surfing traditionally on a longer, wider board meant for noseriding. Young won with his "total involvement" surfing, and that victory is marked as the start of the shortboard revolution. Over the last 40 years, the shortboard has been refined to the **Potato Chip** surfboards of today. Shortboards are generally between 5 feet 6 inches (1.6 meters) and 6 feet 4 inches (2 meters). They are 16 to 19 inches (41 to 48 centimeters) wide, with pointed noses and a variety of tails. Most shortboards are three-finned **Thrusters**, although the single-fin shortboard never goes entirely out of style.

A hyper-kicked, super-thin, super-wide Potato Chip from 1975. This shortboard measures 7 feet 6 inches (2.25 meters). *Fernando Aguerre collection/Juliana Morais*

FOAMBOARD

Also known as **softboards** or **foamies**, these are surfboards ideal for beginners, which have an exterior shell made of soft foam and not hard polyester or epoxy resin. Foamboards float better and are safer than hardboards, and they are generally shaped like longboards or funboards, which makes them the best boards for beginners. There are also shortboards and performance boards made with these softer materials.

Surftech Softop foamboards—the ideal ride for beginners and novices of all types.

TWIN-FIN

A shortboard design using two fins for stability and speed. Twin-fins go back to the 1940s, when they were innovated by Bob Simmons on big balsa wood surfboards. The design became popular in the 1970s, as David Nuuhiwa won the 1972 World Contest on a Fish and Mark Richard developed the twin-fin as a secret weapon he used to win four world titles. Twin-fin surfing is generally more lateral and down the line than vertical surfing.

FUNBOARD

All surfboards are fun, really, but the boards classified as "funboards" can be any size from 5 to 8 feet (1.5 to 2.4 meters) and have longboard qualities: thicker and wider for more flotation and stability, wider tails, and rounder noses. Experienced surfers use these boards when the surf is small—"paddle around, get wet," as they quip—while beginners use them as they are transitioning from longboard to intermediate level.

FISH

During the 1970s, the Fish evolved from kneeboards into a shortboard with two fins, rounded nose, and wide "swallow" tail in lengths anywhere from 5 feet (1.5 meters) to 6 feet 4 inches (2 meters). Fish are great for getting speed in small- to medium-sized waves and are meant to be surfed more laterally, or "down the line," than vertically. Through the 1970s, the Fish begat the **twin-fin**, which inspired the Thruster. In the twenty-first century, Fish are one of the options favored by surfers looking for speed in waves that are small and/or long. First Point Malibu is long and alternately slow and fast, and is considered one of the better waves for Fish in California and the world.

A 1970s Fish with two fins, rounded nose, and wide, "swallow" tail. Such boards are great for getting speed in small- to medium-sized waves and are meant to be surfed more laterally, or "down the line," than vertically.

Zuma Jay displays a clear "funboard" meant for intermediate surfers: "Someone might assume this is the right board, something this size and this shape. But it's not, for a beginner, either. It's too thin. It's way too thin. And it's too narrow in the nose and too hard in the rail."

To Buy or Rent?

Zuma Jay recommends renting your first surfboard to make sure you are going to like surfing and stay with it:

"Rent—don't buy. Try a hardboard; try a softboard. Find out what works for you before you buy a board. That is the best advice I can give to beginners. It's maybe not the smartest thing for my bottom line, but it's honest."

Longboard Sizing Chart

Surfer's Weight (lb)	Surfboard Length
100 to 139	9' 0" to 9' 2"
140 to 159	9' 0" to 9' 4"
160 to 189	9' 4" to 9' 6"
190 to 210	9' 4" to 9' 10"
211 to 235+	10' 0"

Surfer's Weight (kg)	Surfboard Length (cm)
45 to 62	274 to 280
63 to 71	274 to 286
72 to 85	286 to 292
86 to 94	286 to 299
95 to 105+	305

Funboard Sizing Chart

Surfer's Weight (pounds)	Surfboard Length	Surfboard Width	Surfboard Thickness
40 to 60	4' 2"	19.3"	2.3"
65 to 120	5' 8"	20.0"	2.3"
70 to 90	5' 0"	19.3"	2.3"
80 to 140	6' 4"	20.0"	2.7"
100 to 180	7' 5"	21.5"	2.8"
130 to 180	8' 2"	22.0"	3.1"
150 to 230	9' 0"	23.0"	3.1"

Surfer's Weight (kg)	Surfboard Length (cm)	Surfboard Width (cm)	Surfboard Thickness (cm)
18 to 27	125	48.25	5.75
27 to 54	170	50.00	5.75
31 to 40	150	48.25	5.75
36 to 63	190	50.00	6.75
45 to 80	222	53.75	7.00
58 to 80	245	55.00	7.75
67 to 103	270	58.00	7.75

A Fish surfboard is stylish and cool due to the shape and colors on the rail, but Zuma Jay advises that it's not for beginners.

Shortboard Sizing Chart

Surfer's Weight (pounds)	Surfboard Length	Surfboard Width	Surfboard Thickness
100 to 140	6' 2" to 6' 4"	18 ¾" to 19 ¼"	2 ¼" to 2 ⅜"
140 to 160	6' 4" to 6' 8"	19" to 20"	2 3/8" to 2 ½"
160 to 180	6' 6" to 6' 10"	19 ½" to 20 ½"	2 ½" to 2 ⅝"
180 to 200	6' 10" to 7' 4"	20" to 21 ½"	2 ¾" to 3"
200+	7' 4" +	21 ½" to 22 ½"	3" to 3 ¼"

Surfer's Weight (kg)	Surfboard Length (cm)	Surfboard Width (cm)	Surfboard Thickness (cm)
45 to 62	187 to 193	47 to 48	5.70 to 6.00
63 to 71	193 to 203	48 to 50	6.00 to 6.30
72 to 81	198 to 208	48 to 52	6.30 to 6.70
82 to 90	208 to 223	50 to 54	6.90 to 7.60
91+	223 +	54 to 57	7.60 to 8.25

The Hollywood Factor

BLUE CRUSH was a big-budget Hollywood surfing movie released in 2002. It starred Kate Bosworth as Anne Marie Chadwick, a pro surfer with a phobia about Hawaii's famed Pipeline wave. She wiped out there once before, and the memory of hitting her head on a coral reef has given her a scare, a mental barrier she must overcome to achieve her dream of living life as a competitive pro surfer.

Movies like *Blue Crush* and the numerous other Hollywood surf films over the years have a huge influence on novice surfers' visions of the gear they need to surf like the stars. At Zuma Jay's surf shop, he gets many men and women who walk through the front door with no experience who want to do what they saw in the movies, the way they saw it in the movies. "The biggest travesty in surfing are the 'Blue Crush Babes,'" Zuma Jay says.

"These are people who saw the movie and think: 'I'm doing *that*. I'm ready to *go*. I want a board just like she had.' And I say, 'Well, that was Pipe. She was surfing Pipeline.' And they don't understand that the filmmakers used special effects to put Kate Bosworth's face on other stunt surfers."

The Hollywood factor strikes men and women alike. They come into Zuma Jay's shop with surf stars in their eyes, wanting to ride the boards they've seen the pros riding on the big screen or in the magazines. Zuma Jay tries to set them straight: "I always tell the Blue Crush Babes story. You aren't going to surf like her, you aren't even going to paddle like her until you get some muscles going and time going in the water. The skills they saw in an hour-and-a-half movie—it takes years to get to that level."

Zuma Jay shows off a Potato Chip surfboard that's too short and too fast for novices—but is often the first choice of beginners bedazzled by the Hollywood Factor.

Many beginners are drawn toward the shorter, sexier, modern surfboards, but Jay steers them toward the practical: "Even though you may be physically fit, I would still recommend you use a longer board, with thicker rails, for flotation and stability. They might not look as cool on the beach, but you won't spend the day flailing around, not catching waves, and getting frustrated."

continued from page 17
buying a first board is akin to someone going into Victoria's Secret and walking out with new woolen underwear: use common sense.

The first board for most beginners is something big, thick, stable, and practical—not the glamour board that comes later.

"This is what always happens," Zuma Jay says. "You have to let them talk and feel good about what they are telling you. And to do that I let them say, 'Okay, I haven't had any experience but I have a friend who is going to help me.'

"'What did your friend say?' I ask them.

"'Well, my friend said the Kelly Slater board is perfect.'

"And I say, 'Yes, it's perfect—for Kelly Slater. But do you think he

continued on page 28

Zuma Jay explains the virtues of a Surftech Softop "foamboard." Softop boards have a foam core with a hard epoxy layer on the bottom. The parts that may come into contact with your body, however, have a layer of EVA foam for comfort and safety.

The stability of Surftech's Softop foamboards are proven for all time by Malibu surfer Alex Wisemore, who combines her passion for yoga with her passion for the ocean.
Ben Marcus

continued from page 25

started out on a 'Kelly Slater' board? You'll be ready for it in a few years. For now, let's think of something larger that'll be easier for you.'"

Zuma Jay gives beginners an overview of the different kinds of boards. He has witnessed years of transitions in surfboard trends. He began surfing in the 1960s, during the revolution from long boards to shortboards. He was an avid surfer in the 1970s as the shortboard evolved and allowed surfers of his generation more freedom on a wave. "Never in the history of surfing has there been a wider variety of surfboards to ride than today—longboards, shortboards, funboards, hybrids, Fish, and a hundred combinations of all of those. I know it's confusing to beginners, but really I offer them simple advice."

He advises novices to rent their first board, and later he does everything he can to steer them toward buying the right board. But he also encourages beginners to go home, do their research, and shop around, and if they still want to buy or rent from his shop, they are more than welcome.

LENGTH AND WIDTH = HEIGHT, WEIGHT, AND EXPERIENCE

Matching the right surfboard to a beginning surfer is a complex equation with several variables: the surfer's height and weight, and levels of fitness, athletic ability, experience, and commitment.

After all his years in the surfing business, Zuma Jay could be one of those carnival workers who guess the height, weight, and age of anyone who walks up: "When someone walks in who wants to learn to surf, I gauge what I am looking at and make an estimation of their fitness level and what abilities they might have. Are they going to try surfing once, or a couple of times, get frustrated and quit? So when I look at people who come in all wide-eyed, I sum up their physical presence and size them up for a board."

Above all else, Jay steers novices toward the practical—the woolen long johns of the surfboard world. "Even for people who are physically fit, I still recommend they use a longer board, with thicker rails, for flotation and stability. They might not look as cool on the beach, but they won't spend the day flailing around and not catching waves and getting frustrated and quitting."

As he explains, surfers trying to catch their first wave will never catch any wave on a board they can't paddle. "The larger the surface area, the easier it is to stand up."

Psychedelic Colors and Wild Graphics

"When a beginner wants to buy a board, I always recommend they buy something clear, no color," Zuma Jay advises. "The color on a board will cost an extra fifty to one hundred dollars, and why would you spend money on colors for a board when you are going to beat it up and ruin it? If they have that kind of extra money, fine, but for the most part I recommend clear boards."

HARDBOARDS VERSUS SOFTBOARDS

Zuma Jay rents hardboards and softboards and boards that are somewhere in between. The softboard is a concept that goes back to the 1970s, when bodyboard innovator Tom Morey and top waterman Mike Doyle teamed up to produce the **Morey-Doyle surfboard**, a surfboard made of a polyethylene core and skinned with a softer layer of polyethylene bonded to the core. The Morey-Doyle boards were popular with beginners and kids through most of the late twentieth century.

Just before the arrival of the twenty-first century, Santa Cruz board shaper Randy French borrowed techniques from building sailboards to launch a new generation of softboards, known by French's company's name, **Surftech**. French and his board engineers took the softboard concept and improved on it. Surftech's Softop boards have a foam core with a hard-bottomed epoxy layer on the bottom for speed, but the deck and rails have a layer of EVA foam for comfort and safety.

What all that chemical-industrial-complex jargon adds up to is this: Softboards don't do as much damage when they hit your head. The boards are durable and can stand up to all the punishment a beginner can subject them to—but they don't punish the beginner with chipped teeth, bruises, or cuts.

Softboards were initially known as clunky beginner boards that weren't to be taken seriously. But the newest softboards have a hard epoxy layer on the bottom that cuts down on drag and that historical clunkiness. The foam core floats better than traditional polyurethane cores, and the foam wrap on the rails adds up to a board with a great deal of flotation, but that still moves nicely through the water. Softboards are easy to paddle, they catch waves easier, and they move fast and are stable while on a wave.right away."

Surfboard Racks

THERE ARE ALMOST AS MANY STYLES OF surf racks as there are styles of cars. There are hard racks, which mount permanently to cars that have gutters, and there are a wide variety of soft racks. Some racks are custom-made for certain cars, and others have to be improvised.

As Jay warns, "The one thing we don't do is apply straps to the roofs of cars or strap on the surfboards. There is too much liability involved in that, so the customers have to do it themselves, and we encourage them to do it properly: fins forward, wax down, double check them. You don't want your boards flying off on the road—disasters and death have been caused by loose boards flying off cars on the freeway."

A rack stacked full of surfboards atop a VW Beetle.
Jenny Stewart/SurfSister.com

chapter 3

Choosing a Wetsuit and Other Essential Gear

BEGINNING SURFERS LUCKY ENOUGH to be learning in Hawaii, Florida, Indonesia, or southern California in the summer don't have to worry about wetsuits. And even if they are learning at the classic Malibu Beach in springtime, the seasonal northwest winds blow hard and

Left: Since people come in all shapes and sizes—and the ocean flows in a wide variety of temperatures—the variety of wetsuits available is as diverse as the number of surfers. *Phase4Photography/Shutterstock. Right:* Surfing most anywhere from fall to spring means wearing a wetsuit. *Epic Stock/Shutterstock.*

The wrong ways to go surfing. If your goal is to learn to surf in one summer so you can charge Pipeline in Hawaii, think again. Even a brand spanking new Tom Carroll/Phil Byrne Pipeline gun won't get you there. And if your goal is a savage tan thanks to a new bikini from Victoria's Secret, stop right there. A wetsuit is a much better choice for serious surfing.

cause a phenomenon called "upwelling." The winds blow the surface water around and allow colder water to come up from the depths; that colder water inspires the need for more protection than sunscreen, trunks, and rashguards. Spring can be colder than winter in the ocean off California or even Australia. And that can be a shock to people skipping down to the beach in perfect 80-degree weather.

Unless you grew up skinny dipping off the Alaskan coast, for most people, learning to surf anywhere from fall to spring means wearing a wetsuit. And because the ocean flows in a wide variety of temperatures and people come in all shapes and sizes, the variety of wetsuits available is as diverse as the number of surfboard options.

There are more than a dozen companies, large and small, making wetsuits for surfing. Some of these companies are tiny, some are new-

"Wetsuits," then. Movie star and tap dancer Eleanor Powell models the surfing look of the 1930s.

comers, some have been around for a few years. Zuma Jay has been selling O'Neill wetsuits since he opened shop, and he proudly claims to be the largest single-outlet seller of the O'Neill brand in California.

O'Neill is one of the most respected companies in the modern surf industrial complex, in part because it's one of the oldest. The roots of O'Neill wetsuits go back to the 1950s when Jack O'Neill was a park-ing-meter salesman in San Francisco. Working downtown, Jack would make a quick escape to Ocean Beach to bodysurf a few waves and clear his head. Back then, ocean people relied on wool sweaters or just their tough constitution to ward off the cold. O'Neill thought there might be a better way, and he began experimenting with a material he had seen in airplanes: neoprene rubber.

Wetsuits, now. The twenty-first century wetsuit is a miracle of modern science: high-tech neoprene and lining materials combined with computerized stitching and seams. Pro surfer Celine Gerhart prepares to hit the waves at Hossegor, France. *Lucia Griggi*

Jack's experiments with neoprene bunhuggers for bodysurfing lead to neoprene vests for surfing. Jack O'Neill opened the first "surf shop" on the beach in Ocean Beach, and in 1960, he moved his family to Santa Cruz.

What began out of O'Neill's need to literally prevent himself from freezing has become a multi-million-dollar, multinational wetsuit and clothing company. Jack O'Neill's eye-patched head is on every product, but he is as shocked as anyone by all that has happened since 1960. "I was just trying to support my family," Jack says.

O'Neill and Body Glove wetsuits—owned by the Meistrell Brothers—were the leaders in wetsuit innovation during the surf boom of the 1960s. And now 50 years of research and development, innovation, experimentation, and more R&D has evolved into modern wetsuits that are remarkably warm, comfortable, durable, and perfectly designed to give surfers what they want: maximum warmth with maximum performance.

But which brand to choose, which style, which size, which thickness?

The ocean can be shockingly cold in the spring due to the northwest winds. But because summer is coming, the water can go from frigid to semitropical in a couple of weeks. That makes buying a wetsuit a tricky thing, and Zuma Jay recommends that beginners rent wetsuits to see what size and style and thickness they like: fullsuit, spring suit, front zip, back zip, 2 mil, 3 mil, 4 mil.

There is one rule that will generally prove itself always to be true with wetsuits: the more expensive the suit, the warmer it will keep you. That's not to say that you should walk into a surf shop and buy the most expensive model in your size. All suits are meant for different conditions. If you are learning how to catch waves in southern California or Australia in the summertime, you definitely don't need a $500 fullsuit with the best zippers and seams. Choose wisely.

WETSUIT STYLES

There are two basic kinds of wetsuits these days: those with zippers and those without. Different people prefer one over the other, but Jay recommends that beginners go with a zippered wetsuit. The zipper almost always zips up the back.

Beavertail: A beavertail was a wetsuit design that made its debut in the 1970s. The design is the top half of a wetsuit with a frontal zipper and a flap of neoprene that hangs from the back of the suit. This flap was originally meant to be folded through the crotch, latched to the front of the suit, and—the crucial point—worn with **boardshorts**. This design was intended to keep your suit from inch-

Wetsuit Thickness

DENSITY refers to the thickness of the rubber in a wetsuit, commonly measured in millimeters. As common sense would lead you to believe, the suit will keep you warmer if the rubber is thicker. Two numbers are involved in measuring the density of a wetsuit. The most common measurements you'll find in any surf shop are 2/1, 3/2, 4/3, and 5/4. The first number corresponds to the thickness of the neoprene throughout the core of the wetsuit. The smaller second number relates to the neoprene covering your limbs. This difference has been adopted to make it easier for you to move while your body is bound in this form-fitting rubber jumpsuit. Anything below a 2/1 is what we call a **rashguard** and has no notable ability to keep you warm. Anything above a 5/4 is generally reserved for the uneducated, elderly, and the gnarliest of the gnarly who surf in absurdly frigid temperatures.

Left: There are two basic kinds of wetsuits these days: those with zippers and those without. Different people prefer one over the other, but Jay recommends beginners go with a zippered wetsuit. *Right:* Zippered wetsuits almost always have the zip running up the back. Modern wetsuits also come with many other flaps, gaskets, and other widgets that help the back seal up.

ing up your torso, but the tight constriction in the crotch area didn't allow beavertails to progress in the surfing world. If you ever see anyone wearing a beavertail, the infamous piece of neoprene is not clipped but is hanging loose down the backside. It is this aesthetic that gives the suit its name. The general population of beavertail adorners wears these suits for the nostalgic fashion statement, since the flap has no purpose and better wetsuit tops exist. And all that makes beavertails very hip.

Fullsuit: Fullsuits cover your full body. They come in a whole variety of thicknesses but are generally reserved for colder waters and people who get cold really easily. No one wants a whiner out in the lineup.

Short-armed versions do exist, and, not surprisingly, they are called **short-armed fullsuits**.

Long john: A 1970s wetsuit design with a tank-top-like cut on top and long legs. The people who wear beavertails during the summer probably wear long johns in the spring; they're very retro, very hip.

Short john: This style of wetsuit is one of the first worn by surfers with a tank-top-like neck and short legs that end around the lower thigh. It is a *long* john, but with *short* legs. Go figure.

Springsuit: A wetsuit design with short arms and short legs—although spring suits with long arms exist. Springsuits are typically used for cool water and are made of 2/1 millimeter neoprene. The only bummer about spring suits is the nifty farmer tan you inevitably will get on your upper arms and thighs.

Rashguards: Although not technically a wetsuit, if you are looking to buy a wetsuit, you're probably going to take a look into buying a

It's important to know your height and weight, because all of the wetsuit companies have size/weight charts that are particular to their brand to determine sizing. Although the dimensions don't change much from company to company, Zuma Jay uses a chart provided by O'Neill.

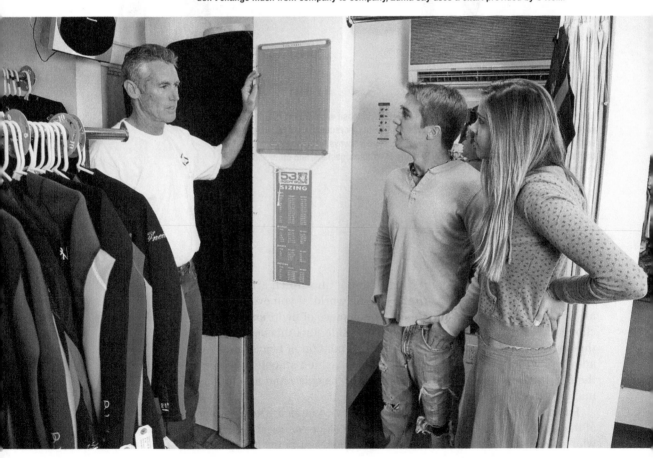

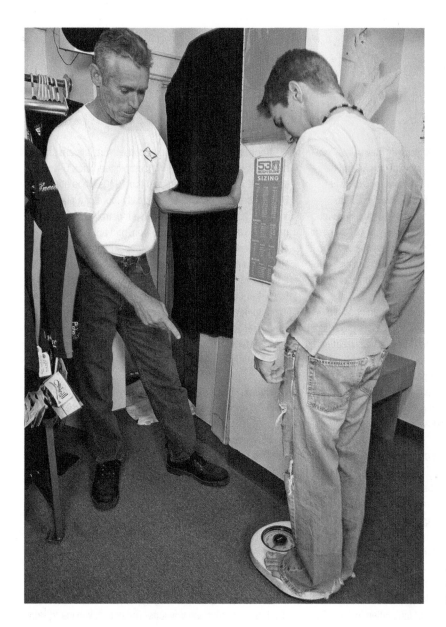

The first step in selecting a wetsuit is to determine your height and weight.

rashguard. These form-fitting shirts are constructed with a nylon-poly-ester-spandex mixture that can be worn under your wetsuit or with just a swimsuit to protect you from chaffing and UV rays during surfing. If you intend to wear them with just a swimsuit, they don't have to be skintight. But if you are getting one to wear beneath your wetsuit, it will only enhance your rash if it is too big. Getting a rash from the fit of your wetsuit or the wax of your board is a common happening, so rashguards are often purchased. But they should not be worn when

continued on page 42

Wetsuit Glossary: Wetsuit Materials and Components

A LOT OF THE TERMS in this glossary may sound like a foreign language to the surf-shop bro working behind the counter. But as a novice surfer, you will want to know what you are shopping for when you go to lay down your hard-earned money for a wetsuit. If you are just learning, any wetsuit within your budget will most likely serve you just fine, and a lot of these terms will simply help you understand why this suit is more expensive than that one. But if you're planning to stick with the sport, you'll want to spend your money well.

Gaskets: These are found around the openings on a wetsuit for your neck, wrists, and ankles. Rubber protrudes from these areas and is folded back into the suit, creating a small rubber trim that inhibits the entrance of water. A lot of companies have quit using gaskets and opt instead for form-fitting rubber. The difference is almost completely undetectable when you are surfing, so don't bother seeking out a gasketed suit for your first wetsuit.

Gusset: The neoprene panel on the arm of a wetsuit.

Kneepads: The patch of rubber on the knee of your wetsuit to keep it from getting torn up from knee-paddling, duck diving, popping up, and other oceanic shenanigans. Different models utilize different types of rubber on their kneepads with the goal of obtaining more flexibility.

Panels: Wetsuits are constructed by binding panels of neoprene together with different kinds of seams. The cut of these panels is an important area of innovation for wetsuit design. Cutting these panels in ways that add to flexibility and limit the amount of seams, and therefore unwanted water entry, is the goal. The fewer panels there are, the less flexible the suit will be, so the invention of more flexible neoprene is fueling this panel-innovation fire.

Jersey: This is the interior of a wetsuit that holds it together and keeps it from falling apart. It is usually constructed out of polypropylene, nylon, titanium, etc. Not necessarily something that needs to be considered when purchasing a suit. Nonetheless, it exists.

Neoprene: This is the material that wetsuits are and have always been made of. Wetsuit pioneer Jack O'Neill stumbled upon the substance in the 1940s while aboard a DC-3 aircraft. Neoprene is technically more of a plastic than a rubber. Its formation has to do with petroleum chips being melted down, compressed into iron, and then being fitted around jersey. What makes neoprene so functional is the "closed-cell" reasoning behind it. Basically, this means that it keeps you warm because it doesn't allow water to flow freely from each of its cells. If you dip a piece of neoprene into a tank of water, only the part that is actually under the water will be wet; the material won't soak up the water like other materials. It's magical—and without it, surfing would not be nearly as enjoyable.

Nylon: Material used for the jersey portion of a wetsuit that was mostly replaced in the 1980s by polypropylene.

Polypropylene: A material used in the jersey of a wetsuit that replaced most nylon jerseys in the 1980s because it has more water resistance. This material can also be found in the insulation of rashguards.

Skin neoprene: A type of neoprene with a laminated layer of nylon, giving it a more rubber-like appearance. Skin neoprene keeps you warmer than average neoprene since the laminated outside is not nearly as porous and therefore doesn't let in as much water. It is also noted for its wind-breaking abilities. High-quality versions are often used to make triathlon wetsuits. The only downside to skin neoprene is its flexibility and durability: it tends to constrict motion and fall apart pretty easily. Most mainstream suits utilize this type of neoprene for the core, leaving the limbs of the suit as normal neoprene for maximum mobility. It is also used for certain gloves, hoods, and booties. But skin neoprene, as well as almost every other component of a wetsuit, is a constant site for innovation. More and more suits are being produced entirely of cutting-edge, flexible skin neoprene. The aesthetic provided by this rubber tends to be a retrospective one, but is also functional—a double whammy of cool.

Stretch or **super-stretch neoprene** is commonly used for the upper portion of a wetsuit to make paddling easier. It is the most flexible neoprene on the market and is beginning to be used to make entire suits. The flexibility of these suits is top-notch in their mobility and fit, but not necessarily their ability to keep water out. These suits will most likely be on the pricier side.

Titanium: A malleable metal occasionally used in neoprene that bounces the surfer's body heat back into the suit—sort of like the greenhouse effect and global warming, just a little more localized and advantageous to humanity.

Velcro: You know Velcro; it was on your shoes before you knew how to tie laces, your fanny pack back in the day, your baseball mitt, and your boardshorts. It's also used on wetsuits in various ways, depending on the design of the suit. It's most commonly used to close up the neck gasket of the suit, but different companies have their way with Velcro in different fashions.

Warranty: A lot of wetsuit manufacturers have warranties on their suits. Some are lifetime deals where if your suit starts to fall apart, you can get a new one for free. Others are only a year long, where the manufacturer will fix up your seams for free for up to a year after you bought the thing. Warranties are something to keep in mind when buying a suit and estimating how long it's going to last you.

ZIPPER STYLES

Asymmetrical zippers: A recent innovation to the common wetsuit zipper. These zippers have staggered teeth, letting less water into your suit than did early zipper styles.

Mini-back zipper or **three-quarter zipper:** A fact to acknowledge is that zippers create a weakness in the force field that is your wetsuit and let water in. This is why **zipperless wetsuits** were created. The problem is, zipperless wetsuits can be a little tricky to slip in and out of. That's why the **mini-zip** was invented. They are shorter and are backed by rubber to fight the battle against water entering your suit uninvited. These were most likely invented for the people who didn't have the flexibility or cardiovascular endurance to wiggle their ways into the zipperless suits.

YKK #10 zipper: This is the basic type of zipper in the wetsuit market. They're as clunky as an eight-track tape, but they get the job done. No fancy whistles and bells with the YKK #10, just closure.

PK-G lock: This is the cream of the zipper crop. Reserved for high-end, cold-water wetsuits with a technology that allows this kind of zipper to be almost completely watertight.

A three-quarter-zip wetsuit, from the pioneering wetsuit maker O'Neill.

Wetsuit Glossary

WETSUIT SEAMS

Seams are the stitching that binds the neoprene panels of a wetsuit together. Seams have been a big focus in the innovation of wetsuits because they generally present a weakness in a suit's ability to keep water out. A multitude of seams have been invented in the heat of this innovation, all with different degrees of effectively keeping water out of your suit.

A wetsuit's seams are all-important, and although you may have never taken any interest in sewing, pay attention now. As Jay explains, "One of things people fail to understand is that the different quality and price of wetsuits are based on the seams. There are stitched seams and glued seams, and there are many different glues and stitches.

"I test the seams by filling up the leg with air and seeing if the air escapes. If the air isn't getting out of the suit, the water won't be going in. When people ask why one suit is $300 and another is $150, I show my seam demonstration. Less air going out means less water getting in, and that means more time for you in the water."

Stress-point taping: If you were to turn a wetsuit inside out, you would see small squares of tape placed on certain points of the seams around the upper-body portion and most of the joints. This is stress-point taping. Its job is to keep your suit as durable as possible without inhibiting its mobility. Once you've had your first suit for a couple of years and it starts getting holes in all of its corners, you will understand why stress-point taping exists. Most suits have stress-point taping, but even so, it may do little to combat the wear and tear a diligent surfer can put a suit through.

Taped seams: A type of sealing tape used to cover up a seam's stitching. Back in the day, taped seams were the cutting edge of wetsuit technology. It has since been outgrown by the flexibility of liquid seam tape (like the stuff used in glued blind stitching). When it is used now at all it's most likely in certain vulnerable areas of the suit (like in stress-point taping).

Flat-stitched seam or **flat-locked seam:** A type of stitching that goes completely through both sides of the neoprene, lays flat, and has the appearance of railroad tracks. Wetsuits with this type of stitching will generally be less expensive, since no crazy technology is involved

in their construction. More water will be let in through these seams than through wetsuits with glued seams. Flat-stitched suits are best for summertime surfing, fiscally challenged surfers, and beginners who don't want to invest too much money into their newfound hobby just yet.

Blind-stitched seam: A type of seam where the two neoprene panels it conjoins are first glued together and then sewn, but only halfway through. Without the thread puncturing all the way to the other surface of neoprene, less water is let into the suit. This type of stitching is found on higher-end wetsuits and is fairly durable and watertight at this point.

Like the blind-stitched seam, the **double-blind-stitched seam** utilizes the idea that if you glue the seam together first and only stitch the thread halfway through the neoprene, less water will get in. But unlike the average blind-stitched seam, the double-blind-stitched seam blind stitches the outside of the suit (with the thread only going halfway through the rubber), turns the suit inside out, and does it again from the inside of the suit. As you can imag-

Left: Zuma Jay's Blow-Up Trick for wetsuits to show the importance of good-quality seams. He explains: "One of things people fail to understand is that the different quality and price of wetsuits are based on the seams. There are stitched seams and glued seams and there are many different glues and stitches. I test the seams by filling up the leg with air and seeing if the air escapes."
Right: If the air can't get out of the suit, the water won't get in. Zuma Jay says, "When people ask why one suit is three hundred dollars and another is one hundred fifty dollars, I show my seam demonstration. Less air going out means less water getting in, and that means more time in the water."

ine, this innovation allows for even less water getting into a suit than does the average blind-stitch seam.

Glued-and-blind-stitched (GBS) seams: Just like the name makes it sound, GBS seams are both glued and blind-stitched, making them even more watertight than both the blind-stitched and double-blind-stitched seams.

A **sealed-and-taped seam** is a glued, blind-stitched seam that also has interior taping along the seams. This tape is usually made up of a type of rubber or neoprene and adds to the durability and watertight aspect of the suit and its seams.

Expanded Seam Technology (EST): EST is the seam that isn't really a seam at all. Pieces of neoprene are woven together and then covered in flexible rubber glue, making the suit incredibly watertight and flexible. This technique gives this non-seam a wave-like appearance. The technology is often noted for its ability to have pressure applied to it from any direction. People have experimented to see how far these things will stretch without having anything bad happen to the suit. That being said, don't try it. Companies sometimes advertise their use of EST technology by calling a suit "stitchless." In the battle against the unavoidable entrance of water into your suit that stitches provide, as opposed to going the popular "seamless" route—trying to make a suit with the smallest amount of seam work—EST goes for the "stitchless." Very clever indeed.

continued from page 37

you are not taking part in an aquatic activity. They may seem cool, but they are not a successful fashion statement.

An **insulated rashguard** features a polypropylene lining to keep you a bit warmer than the average rashguard.

A **zipperless wetsuit**, as you might guess, is a wetsuit that doesn't have any zippers. Instead, it uses a lot of super-stretch neoprene. These suits are more watertight since they don't have to deal with the amount of water that inevitably creeps in through a zipper. These warm and stretchy suits are a little tricky to get into, though, and they have a short lifespan since super-stretch neoprene isn't the most durable material. The only real bummer about zipperless wetsuits is the series of convoluted yoga moves you have to do to get into them. But if that just sounds like a nice pre-surf warmup to you, zipperless might be the way to go.

WETSUIT SIZING

The first step in sizing a wetsuit is to determine your height and weight. It's important to know height and weight, because all wetsuit companies have size charts that are particular to their brand, although the basic dimensions don't change much from company to company.

Modern wetsuits come with lots of flaps, gaskets, and other widgets that help the back seal up—and sometimes that process requires assistance.

The Plastic Bag Trick

For putting on a wetsuit, Zuma Jay offers a trick: a simple plastic bag. Place a plastic bag on your feet or hands when trying on wetsuits and they slide on much faster.

RASHGUARDS

Rashguards serve two purposes: they provide sun and rash protection when you aren't wearing a wetsuit and warmth and chafing protection when you are wearing a wetsuit. "The first thing I ask when people ask about rashguards is: 'What are you using it for?'" Zuma Jay says. "If you aren't wearing a wetsuit, you want to protect yourself from too much sun, but also chafing from sand in the wax—and the decks of the Softop surfboards can also chew up your chest and your skin. Surfing without a wetsuit is a little more comfortable with a rashguard."

Although wetsuits are light-years better than they were in the 1970s, they still can chafe and cause rashes, and mixing rashes with saltwater can be uncomfortable and drive you from the water.

Rashguards come in different thicknesses, as well as long-sleeve, short-sleeve, and hooded models. There are rashguards made with UV sun protection ratings. Some are lycra, others a neoprene mix.

"I stock O'Neill rashguards because I am O'Loyal," Zuma Jay says, "and they seem to be a leading innovator in making rashguards that are stronger, warmer, more comfortable. You can use the same rashguard under a wetsuit or not under a wetsuit. The differences are subtle. So once we figure out what beginners will be using the rashguard for, we go from there: Try them on, see what feels good, looks good."

Just don't wear rashguards to clubs or whatever. It looks dumb and they make you sweat.

SURF TRUNKS

The market for surf trunks is worth hundreds of millions of dollars, and the companies that now dominate the surf industry—Billabong and Quiksilver—both started by making surf trunks. The size and value of that market inspires a great deal of innovation and competition. Zuma Jay ignores most of it: "For the hardcore people we stock Birdwell and the Katin: No fancy colors, no fancy gimmicks. Decent quality with a liner. Very durable, but they dry quickly and fit nicely under the wetsuit. Katins and Birdwells are what we call: 'Three inches [7½ centimeters] above the knee.' The right length, but not looking 1960s or 1970s. Katin and Birdwell are more traditional trunks, but I like them and they are made in America, and I like that.

"For the high-tech people who want the latest, greatest thing they can talk about and show off on the beach we've got O'Neill shorts. O'Neill has been a leader in wetsuit neoprene technology and they have also applied that kind of technology to surf trunks. The new surf trunks are very high-tech: materials, seams, pockets, liners—everything."

Ultimately, however, your choice of surf trunks should be based on fit. As Jay says, "The best advice I can give to people is to shop around, try them on, see what fits, what looks good, what feels good. There is a lot to choose from and it all comes down to personal taste."

Webbed gloves are ideal for cold-temperature surfing and for paddling into big waves.

GLOVES

Gloves are generally used by the uneducated, elderly, and gnarly who are surfing in extremely cold temperatures and massive surf (these are the same surfers wearing wetsuits thicker than 5/4). Even though webbed gloves seem like a clever idea, they have been known to strain your back muscles if worn every session in average-size waves—although some big-wave surfers swear by them for that extra kick over the ledge. Gloves are generally unnecessary—unless you fall under the previously mentioned "gnarly" category.

FINS

Fins are made to cut through the water and provide directional stability while not sacrificing speed. That means fins are foiled and sharp, and they can do damage. These days there are a wide variety of fin choices for every possible situation, but for beginners, the accent should be on safety first and everything else second: "If beginners are having a real hard time we give them the padded fins, like Pro Teck," Zuma Jay says. "They have a thin layer of padding on the leading edge and on the back. When the beginners are a little better and are aware of fin cuts and ankle cuts, we move them down to the smaller, more dynamic fins, like honeycomb stuff."

Talk the Talk

In surf lingo, **gnarly** is usually something so "bad" that it's "good"—for instance, a wave so big and intimidating that it's awesome. The shortened—and cooler form—is **gnar**. Something that's gnarly to the maximum degree and can't get any cooler is **gnarmax**.

BOOTIES

A pair of booties will protect your feet from rocks, broken glass, squishy sea slugs, stingrays, and all the animals, vegetables, and minerals your feet are likely to encounter while shuffling across the ocean floor. Beginning surfers entering the ocean for the first time have enough to worry about on the surface of the ocean and don't need to be distracted by where their feet are going as well.

Even on sandy beaches there is a danger of stepping on a stingray, which is something you *really* don't want to do. So for beginners who want to focus on getting their feet onto a surfboard, wetsuit booties are a good idea: "If beginners are going to Surfrider or Sunset or some other rocky point break, I recommend they wear booties," Zuma Jay says. "Booties are helpful over rocky bottoms. There are high tops, low tops, split toe, no toe. Expensive booties, cheaper booties. I tell people to try them on and see what they like."

If it's too warm for booties, there are also various brands of reef shoes, reef sandals, and reef walkers that are made of lighter material than neoprene and still provide protection.

Sandals won't work. All you will do is trip over your feet and fall.

Booties protect your feet from rocks, broken glass, stingrays, and everything else on the ocean floor.

HELMETS

Consider the credo of famed big-wave surfer Roger Erickson: "Everything's okay until it isn't." Anyone who has been surfing for a few years

If you're not entirely comfortable with the thought of going surfing, a helmet is a good choice.

Being over-prepared—with a wetsuit, helmet, waterproof sunglasses, booties, and webbed paddling gloves—is a good idea for a beginner surfer. As you become more confident and lose your inhibitions, you can also lose the extra gear.

will have stories of injuries that come from out of nowhere—and when they least expect them.

Some beginners might feel safer wearing a helmet made specifically for surfing; others might feel goofy. Wearing the helmet is the good decision.

HOODS

That old wives' tale we've all heard—how 90 percent of your body heat escapes from your head—is true, and the difference between wearing a hood or not will prove this. A hood can mean the difference between shivering during the lulls and being toasty on the outside. Although hoods are not necessary year-round, they can be extremely efficient when they are.

Hoods are made of a neoprene softer than that of the rest of your suit and cover your entire head up to under your nose if you find the right model. They can be detachable from your suit, permanently attached, or a separate entity completely.

chapter 4

Surfing 101:
The Dry Run

CHARGING CLUELESSLY OUT INTO THE OCEAN to catch your first wave is not a safe practice. You should first begin on the beach, practicing surfing technique: learning about balance and stability, how to paddle, how to pop up on the board, and how to stand and ride a wave. This is truly the dry run.

Left: Mircea Bezergheanu/Shutterstock. Right: Good surfing starts here, on the beach. Practicing your positioning, paddling, and popping up before you even hit the waves is the way to get it right.

Carla Rowland hangs five at Malibu, ready for whatever.
Ian Zamora

The best route to get up and surfing is to surf with an experienced friend or hire an instructor. Zuma Jay has been sizing up beginners for more than 30 years, and he has answered the same questions 10,000 times: "Most beginners walk in with that same look of innocence, bewilderment, and eagerness," Jay says. "They want to learn to surf, but have no clue where to start. The first thing I do is ask if they have any experience. If they say, 'No, no, and no,' I then ask if they have ever had a lesson. If they say, 'No, I'm just starting out,' then I suggest they have a lesson or two with an experienced surfer.

"It's easier to have a friend who will dedicate a couple of hours to it. Buy your buddy a dinner. But I recommend they go with someone who will teach rather than show: 'Watch how I do this. Watch how I do that. See how I did that?'"

Zuma Jay believes the investment of buying a buddy dinner or in hiring a surf instructor is worthwhile, but he also knows that it's an expense most beginners didn't factor in to their calculations of the costs of learning to surf. Money is always tight, so justify this added expense by saving money on equipment and investing it in an hour, a day, or several days of instruction.

Carla Rowland is a surf instructor based at California's famed Malibu Beach. She's been a regular at Malibu going back to childhood when her dad, Wayne, first took her into the water at the age of the seven. Over the years, influenced by her dad and by all the great surfers who have ridden Malibu from the 1980s into the twenty-first century, Carla has become one of the best surfers in the lineup, male or female.

Beginning in 1999, she has held private and group lessons for local citizens and visitors who want to learn the secrets of the sea: "I've been surf instructing for ten years and I've seen all the goods and bads. I've seen all the mistakes, and made a few myself."

Carla handles individuals and small groups, becoming part lifeguard, part psychiatrist—encouraging the shy and the clumsy and the overconfident in the proper ways to approach the ocean with a surfboard: "A lot of the people I instruct are experiencing the ocean for the first time. I have been around the ocean all my life and it's second nature to me. A lot of the students I work with don't have that generational attachment. They've moved here from Wisconsin or are visiting, they saw *Blue Crush* or some other movie and they thought: 'I want to try that.' Many of my students have no California or ocean background and they are as green as you can get."

That greenness begins with surfers arriving at the beach with their boards strapped to the roof, wax up, melting in the sun, and it goes from there: "Beginners putting their wetsuits on backward—that's common," Carla says: "They come out of the bathroom with the zipper in the front, zipped up to their necks."

Carla believes her seven-year experience as a special education special assistant gave her the skills to deal with the beginning surfers who come to her for wisdom: "I pride myself on being a very detailed instructor," she says. "And as someone who worked as a special education special assistant for seven years, I know there is a rainbow of intelligences out there—and that also applies to physical intelligence. My job is to figure out where on that spectrum my students are and then push them. Some need gentle coaxing, some fly out of the nest right away."

Carla charges anywhere from $80 to $120 for a two-hour lesson. She admits that some students hesitate at the price, but she believes the investment will save beginners hundreds of hours in frustration: "Everything I have learned I have learned from my father, as well as other surfers on the beach. I know when I started surfing, I was awkward and I didn't like being awkward, but I got a lot of positive reinforcement from my dad and the Malibu guys. So I try to give my students a lot of positive reinforcement, to the point of being overly encouraging."

She begins with a dry run on the beach—15 to 30 minutes of Surfing 101 instruction: "I tell them the basics: There will be a lot of paddling. The objective is to ride closest to the curl. And always protect yourself."

STRETCHING

"Always protect yourself" covers a lot things for beginning surfers. One of the items surfers need to protect themselves from is injury. Carla says, "I tell all beginners they will be using muscles they never knew they had, in ways they never have before. I always stretch to limber up before surfing, and I encourage my students to do the same."

Left: One of the things surfers need to protect themselves from is injury, including muscle cramps. Carla says: "I tell all beginners they will be using muscles they never knew they had, in ways they never have before. I always stretch to limber up before surfing, and I encourage my students to do the same."

Below: Surfing is hard on the spine, hard on the joints, and demands a lot from the hips. Carla warns: "Whatever you've got, stretch it and get it loose, because you are going to need it."

Left: Surfers overdevelop muscles in their arms, back, and neck. "This beginner has nice guns," Carla points out. "But he is going to be shooting them in new ways."

Below: Even if you're in good shape, stretching is essential. If surfing is a new sport to you, you'll want your muscles ready for anything.

Surfing, at best, is about 70 percent paddling, 20 percent waiting and getting in position, and 10 percent actually being up and riding. Surfers overdevelop muscles in their arms and back and neck from the paddling. But Carla warns, "whatever you've got, stretch it and get it loose, because you are going to need it."

KNOWING YOUR SURFBOARD

Regardless of whether you're learning to surf on a traditional hardboard or a Softop, they both have basic things in common: a deck, a bottom, rails, a nose, and a tail.

The Importance of Paddling

Surfing is 70 percent paddling;
20 percent waiting and getting in position;
and 10 percent actually being up and riding.

Paddling a surfboard and sitting on a surfboard and leaping to your feet puts a lot of strain on the lower back. "It's good to loosen it up," Carla says. "A lot of people can't go to their toes, but I tell them to go as low as they can."

Carla teaches on both traditional hardboards and Softops, but regardless of the materials and construction of the surfboard, they all have things in common: Deck, bottom, rails, nose, tail. Beginning with the basics, Carla shows the top of the board and explains that most surfers call it the "deck." The sides of the board that cut through the water are the "rails."

Talk the Talk

The top of a surfboard is the **deck**. This is where the wax goes and where a surfer lies while paddling and stands while riding.

It may seem blindingly obvious, but the deck of the board should stay sunny-side up; it's where you ride. The bottom of the board, with the fin or fins, goes ocean-side down. The nose of the board goes to the front; the tail, with the fin below, goes to the back. Carla says, "I have never had anyone paddle a board fin up, but I have heard of that happening."

Learning to surf is all about subtle shifts in weight. When paddling for a wave, it is best to be in the middle of the board, to get the best balance and get the most speed and planning out of the board. When you catch a wave, there will be forward momentum, so it's necessary to shift your weight back until you are riding the wave. Then the best balance point is forward again, in the middle or up toward the nose, depending on the wave.

Above: The nose of the board goes forward, Carla says, as she stands at the tail and points toward the nose.

The fin is on the bottom of the board and points down in the water.

Fin-First Takeoffs

Malibu is home to some of the best longboard surfers in the world, tricksters who hang five, hang ten, hang heels. Some of the Malibu surfers like to do fin-first takeoffs in which they stand on the board tail forward, the fin digs in and the surfboard spins 180 degrees as the surfer tries to keep his balance and forward momentum.

SURFBOARD STANCE

In surf lingo, a **regular foot** is a surfer who rides with their left leg forward. A **goofy foot** surfs with their right leg forward. Your surfboard stance has nothing to do with being right- or left-handed, and it doesn't appear to be hereditary either. Carla is naturally a goofy foot, but you wouldn't know that half the time as she has mastered the art of **switching foot**, which means she can ride a wave with either foot forward. It's something Carla uses for speed and positioning at Malibu, but that is an advanced technique that is far in the future for anyone learning to surf.

"When determining the stance of a surfer I ask for previous history. Most students have ridden a skateboard or a snowboard or a wakeboard and so they know what their stance is. It's pretty rare to have someone who has never been on a board. But when that happens, what I do is have them

Softops are not Soft

The rails on a Softop surfboard are nearly as hard as the rails on a hardboard, and they will hurt if they bonk you. To her students, Carla warns, "Always protect yourself."

The Fall Forward Test

Stand with your feet together, then fall forward. Whichever leg you use to catch yourself will usually be the forward leg for your stance.

You need to determine which stance you should use—regular foot (left leg forward) or goofy foot (right leg forward). Use the Fall Forward Test: Stand with your feet together, then fall forward. Whichever leg you use to catch yourself will usually be your forward leg for your stance. Stance has nothing to do with being right handed or left handed, and it doesn't appear to be hereditary either.

A goofy foot surfer rides with their right foot forward; thus, the leash straps to your back, or left, leg.

A regular foot surfer wears the leash on their back, or right, foot.

stand with their feet together then fall forward, and whatever leg they use to catch themselves, that is usually their stance."

But that doesn't always work. Sometimes people who snowboard in one stance will surf in the other. And the Fall Forward Test sometimes falls apart when beginners get out in the water and get to their feet.

"Stance is important for figuring out which leg the leash attaches to," Carla says. "Sometimes I get them in the water with a leash on one foot and on their first wave they will stand the other way. Stance is something that evolves. It can require leash switching occasionally, but we figure it out."

PADDLING POSITION

If surfing is 70 percent paddling, then good paddling technique can make the difference between success and failure. "In my experience, most beginners are surprised by how much paddling is involved," Carla says. "Not just to catch the wave, but to get into position and stay in position: The lineup is changing, the current is moving."

Learning to surf is a matter of subtle weight adjustments, and almost everything in surfing is done from the middle of the board. "Finding your ideal position on the board for paddling has a lot to do with your board, you, and the ocean conditions," Carla explains. "Finding that position evolves, like finding your stance."

If you're too far forward on your board while paddling, your board would dive underwater—and so would you, if a wave came along. Surfers call this **pearling** from "pearl diving."

The opposite of pearling is **bogging**. Here, your weight is distributed too far back, the board can't plane or get any speed, and waves just wash over the board, bogging the board.

To paddle properly, you need to be in the middle of your board. Carla says, "I teach my students to extend their arms and make fluid strokes stretching all the way out and back. The key is to get into a graceful motion, where your arms are moving and the board is moving and it's all working together. Don't shake side to side."

Some beginners will try the simultaneous paddling method, stroking both arms at the same time. That style is more common to longboards and in days of old, but Carla says it's OK: "Two-arm paddle breaks up the monotony, but it's not always the fastest method for catching waves."

Paddling with your hand open is far less efficient than with your hand closed. Paddle with your fingers together and cupped, just like you swim.

Talk the Talk

The **lineup** is the spot in the water where surfers "line up" to catch a wave just outside where the waves break. A group of approaching waves is called the **set**. The **breakline** is the point in the lineup where the waves begin to break.

Paddling Position

The correct paddling position is chest up with the lower back arched.

Talk the Talk

Pearling is taken from "pearl diving," and it's what happens when a surfer's weight is too far forward and the nose of the board dives underwater.

Your surfboard is **bogged** when waves wash over it.

Paddling while laying too close to the nose of your board, like this, is the proper position only for disaster, embarrassment, and getting a close-up look at the ocean bottom, but not for catching waves. The nose of the board will dive under. Surfers call this "pearling."

If your weight is too far back, as here, the board can't plane or get speed, and the water will wash over the board, "bogging" it.

Here, the paddlers have their bodies just right. They are in the middle of their boards, and they've got both arms going. In the water, they would be moving along nicely to get into position to catch a wave.

The correct paddling position is to keep your chest up with your lower back arched.

Keep your legs together as you paddle, too. Paddling with legs splayed apart is as inefficient as paddling with fingers spread. You want a tight, sleek profile when paddling, and if your legs are together you won't rock back and forth.

Also, keep your feet out of the water. Having feet drag in the water is like putting on the brakes. You want all the speed you can get while paddling, so keep your legs in close.

Most first-timers find paddling uncomfortable and so they slog along, shoulders and chest and neck down, face pressed into the board, unable to see where they are going, or what is coming at them.

Proper paddling form is to arch your lower back, and have your chest and neck and head up and aware as you stroke along smoothly, prowling like a cheetah, moving through the water like a barracuda.

Paddle smooth like a cheetah, fast like a barracuda.

Knee Paddling

Paddling while kneeling is an advanced technique, but some people get it right off. It's more comfortable, and warmer. Knee paddling provides elevation and lets you see waves coming before the prone paddlers see them. Some beginners take to knee paddling right away, some don't.

Left: Do not paddle with your fingers spread wide. Open-handed paddling is far less efficient than close-handed. *Right:* You can't ride a wave until you catch a wave, and you aren't going to catch a wave until you can paddle efficiently. Paddling with fingers together and cupped is the way.

Keep your legs together. Paddling with your legs splayed apart is as inefficient as paddling with fingers spread. You want a tight, sleek profile when paddling, and if your legs are together you won't rock back and forth.

Keeping your legs together is good advice for efficient paddling and surfing.

Dragging your feet out in the water is like putting on the brakes. You want all the speed you can get while paddling, so keep your legs in close.

Many beginners find paddling uncomfortable and difficult, so they naturally put their shoulders, chest, and neck down, face pressed into the board, unable to see where they are going.

Lift your chest above the board to stroke along smoothly.

Knee paddling is more comfortable—and it's warmer when water temperatures are low. Knee paddling provides elevation and lets you see waves coming before the prone paddlers.

PUSHING THROUGH A WAVE

Beginning surfers confronted by a breaking wave can try a number of ways to get past it and suffer the least interruption: **turning turtle**, **bailing out**, and **pushing through**.

Because beginners are ideally learning in small surf, pushing through usually works best. When paddling along and a breaking wave or a line of foam is coming at you, the best defense is to raise up on the board and put as much space between you and the board, let the wave or foam pass under and around you. The key to a proper push through is to lift your *whole* body off the board.

Talk the Talk

Turning turtle is a surfing technique where the surfer flips the surfboard over in front of an oncoming wave to get under it. It's usually done with a longboard instead of duck diving, which is especially difficult with a longboard.

When paddling out, you can push through incoming breaking waves by raising yourself up on the board, letting the wave or foam pass under and around you.

The correct posture for pushing through a wave is like doing a full-body push-up on your surfboard.

Duck Diving

Duck diving is the fine art of pushing the board under and through a breaking wave and getting through the back of the wave without going "over the falls." Duck diving done properly is a combination of water ballet and water polo, but that is an advanced technique for experienced surfers.

Bailing

Letting go of your surfboard—also known as **bailing**—is generally considered a no-no. If you bail, you're in trouble, as you won't have your bouyant board to keep you afloat. Letting go of your board can lead to injury to yourself, but also to others behind you if your board strikes them or they run into it. Still, sometimes there is no other choice but to bail.

The key to pushing through a wave properly is to lift your *whole* body off the surfboard.

POPPING UP AND STANDING

Some beginner surfers choose to ride waves prone first, then get to their knees; when they feel comfortable on their knees, they work their way up to standing. This can work fine. But Carla recommends not riding waves on your knees: "I think encouraging beginners to use their knees is encouraging a bad habit, a crutch. I make my students believe that once they have caught the wave, they should stand right away. And the best way to do that is in one fluid motion."

When you're ready to **pop up**, use as much upper body strength as you can muster in order to get your feet underneath you as quickly as possible. Rotate your front hip so that your front foot is in front. Don't stand parallel; you'll lack your sense of balance. Keep your feet spread out enough to be stable. Not too narrow.

Do not stand too far back on the tail. Even if you were an experienced surfer and were about to whip a giant bottom turn, you need to be careful still about being too far back onto the tail. For a beginner, standing on the tail would bog the board.

As Carla explains: "The board is most maneuverable when standing above the tail on the fin, but that also slows the board down. As you progress you will learn to transfer your weight from the tail to the center in order to maximize your ride."

While it is too early to talk about good surfing style, now that you are standing, your arms are no longer your propulsion mechanisms, but your all-important balance points. On any wave, you will be buffeted by the moving water and perhaps the wind. Use your arms to balance. Still, in general, while surfing it is considered good style to keep your arms at waist level or lower. Waving your arms around is not good style; that's called "flailing"—and for obvious reason.

Your knees are also essential to your balance. Bend your knees: they are your shock aborbers. Carla explains: "Don't forget to bend those knees. Once you are up and riding, your knees are as important as your arms for balance.

Talk the Talk

Popping up is the quick move a surfer makes to rise to a standing position when taking off on a wave.

Standing Tip

If you're in the correct paddling position—chest up with the lower back arched—the transition from prone to standing will be much smoother.

Arm Positioning

For good surfing style, keep your arms at waist level or lower. This will also help your balance on the board.

To pop up and stand on your board, you need to move quickly and strongly.

Use as much upper-body strength as you can muster in order to get your feet underneath you—fast.

The correct paddling position is chest up, lower back arched—and if you do that correctly, the transition from prone to standing is much smoother.

Rotate your front hip so that your front foot is in front. Don't stand with your feet parallel to each other.

Keep your feet spread out wide enough to be stable. Bend your knees, as they are your shock absorbers and will aid your balance.

Viewed from the side, move with quickness and determination to pop up and stand.

You want your feet underneath your body as quickly as possible; use as much upper-body strength as you can muster to move fast.

If you are in the correct paddling position—your chest up and lower back arched—the transition from prone to standing is much smoother.

Good surfing style dictates keeping your arms at waist level or below. Your arms are now your balance points.

If you stand too far back on the tail, as here, you'll bog the board, make it slow down, and all that grace you showed getting to your feet would be wasted as you wipe out.

Right: With too much strength, it's possible to pop up—and do an instant backflip. Learning to keep your balance and control the popup is key.

Below Left: As a beginner, you may pop up and find yourself a little off-balance and a little too far back on the tail, as shown here. But keep low, in a crouch, with your knees bent and back flexible, and you can overcome the positioning.

Below Right: Keeping your knees bent is all-important in standing. "Don't forget to bend your knees," Carla says. "Once you are up and riding, your knees are as important as your arms for balance."

Left: Riding too far back on the board, as here, will result in the board bogging. Carla says: "The board is most maneuverable when standing above the tail on the fin, but that also slows the board down."

Below Left: As you get your footing, rotate your front hip so that your front foot is in front.

Below Right: Keeping your balance is all in your knees, arms, weight distribution, and your position on the board. Carla explains: "As you progress you will learn to transfer your weight from the tail to the center in order to maximize your ride."

chapter 5

Into the Water

HOW TO CHOOSE THE BEST BEGINNER SURFING SPOTS

The ideal surf spot for beginners has long, gentle waves breaking for a good distance over a wide, sandy beach. Warm water is better than cold, because it's easier to stay out in warm water—and learning to surf is all about water time and experience as much as balance or nerve. If the warm waters and those long, gentle waves over a wide, sandy beach are protected from winds and currents and other nastiness by a headland, point, pier, jetty, or other obstruction, that is good news, too.

Left: Your first successful surf session will have you all smiles. *Epic Stock/Shutterstock*
Right: For beginner surfers, the ideal spot has long, gentle waves breaking over a good distance on a wide, sandy beach, such as here at California's Zuma Beach.

Best Beginner Beaches Worldwide

THIS IS JUST A PARTIAL LIST of some of the best beaches for beginner surfers. For a more thorough list—as well as surf instruction at each beach—see the appendix.

WEST COAST AND HAWAIIAN ISLANDS
Waikiki Beach, South Shore, Oahu, Hawaii
Launiupoko, Maui, Hawaii
Hanalei, North Shore, Kauai, Hawaii
Linda Mar, Pacifica, California
Cowell's Beach, Lighthouse Point, Santa Cruz, California
Mondos, Faria Point, Ventura County, California
Surfrider Beach, Malibu, California
San Onofre State Park, San Clemente, California
Tourmaline Surfing Park, San Diego, California
La Jolla Shores, La Jolla, California
Frank Island, Tofino, British Columbia, Canada

EAST COAST AND THE GULF
South Padre Island, Texas
Galveston, Texas
Cocoa Beach, Florida
Virginia Beach, Virginia
Folly Beach, South Carolina
Outer Banks, North Carolina
Wrightsville Beach, North Carolina
Ocean City, Maryland
Sea Isle City, New Jersey
Robert Moses State Park, New York
Nantucket, Massachusetts
Coast Guard Beach, Cape Cod National Seashore, Massachusetts
Narragansett Town Beach, Rhode Island
Jenness Beach, Rye, New Hampshire
Oqunquit, Maine
York, Maine

AUSTRALIA AND NEW ZEALAND
Noosa Head, Queensland
Currumbin Beach, Gold Coast, Queensland
Greenmount Beach, Coolangatta, Gold Coast, Queensland
Surfer's Paradise, Gold Coast, Queensland
Rainbow Bay, Gold Coast, Queensland
Byron Bay, New South Wales
South Palm Beach, Sydney, New South Wales
Manly, Sydney, New South Wales
Cronulla, Sydney, New South Wales
Fisherman's Beach, Torquay, Victoria
Torquay Main Beach, Victoria
Scarborough Beach, Perth, Western Australia
Auckland, New Zealand
Mount Maunganui, New Zealand
Raglan, New Zealand

MEXICO AND THE CARIBBEAN
Jaco Beach and Playa Hermosa, Costa Rica
Nosara, Costa Rica
Playa Dominical, Costa Rica
Playa Guiones, Nicoya Peninsula, Costa Rica
Tamarindo, Costa Rica
Cabo San Lucas, Mexico
Barras de Piaxtla, Mazatlan, Sinaloa, Mexico
Playa Troncones, Zihuatenejo, Mexico
Mazatlan and Puerto Vallarta, Mexico
Punta de Mita, Nayarit, Mexico
Puerto Escondido, Mexico
Rincon, Puerto Rico

THE REST OF THE WORLD
Surfer's Point, Barbados
Itacare, Bahia
Rio de Janeiro, Brazil
Florianopolis, Brazil
Sedgewell Cove, Bigbury-on-Sea, South Devon, England
Newquay, Cornwall, England
Polzeath, Cornwall, England
Croyde, North Devon, England
Biarritz, France
Hossegor, France
Lacanau, France
Seignosse, France
Kugenuma Beach, Shonan, Japan
Muizenberg, Cape Town, South Africa
Jeffreys Bay, Eastern Cape, South Africa
Port Elizabeth, Eastern Cape, South Africa
East London, Eastern Cape, South Africa
Durban, KwaZulu-Natal, South Africa

Finding a beginning surf spot where there are few experienced surfers reigning over the waves is also essential. *Lucia Griggi*

The Sticky Business of Surf Wax

SURF WAX is essentially a petroleum byproduct—based on paraffin, the first byproduct to be separated in the processing of crude oil—but it's essential to surfing. Waxing the top of your surfboard is the key to retaining your traction on the board in the wet.

There isn't a lot of science to surf wax. And yet there are dozens of brands of wax in a variety of fruit flavors and colors for a variety of conditions, from cold to cool to warm to tropical. In choosing a wax, simply look at the labels and find the temperature range they are meant for. Cold-water waxes are formulated to go on easier because they don't have the heat to make them liquid. But if you use a cool- or cold-water wax in tropical waters, you will leave a layer of oil in the water behind you—and possibly attract the ire of Greenpeace.

There are also **base coat** and **top coat** waxes. Some surfers will lay down a specially formulated base of harder wax, which creates a layer of traction. On top of that, a different formulation of wax provides traction and sure footing.

A bar of wax costs around $1, so buy a couple: hand them to friends, or to a stranger and make them a friend. But once you buy the wax, be careful with it. Follow these commandments below to assure peace, tranquility, and traction.

THE 10 COMMANDMENTS OF SURF WAX

1. Skiers wax for speed; surfers wax for traction. For surfing, wax the top of the surfboard.

2. Thou shall keep sand and rocks out of your wax.

3. Thou shall not strap your boards to the roof of the car wax-side up. Otherwise, you'll have melted goo all over the roof of your ride.

4. Wax is good for temporary ding repairs.

5. Buy a wax container and use it. Melted surf wax in clothing, glove boxes, car seats, and hair can lead to depreciation and divorce.

6. Thou shall remove old wax with foam dust and then acetone. Just melting it off works, but is bad for your board.

7. When thou uses surf wax to create graffiti or warn away outsiders, thou shall use proper diction and spelling.

8. Thou shall not covet thine own wax. Always share it. They'll make more.

9. Do not eat surf wax. Yes, it smells good, but so do roses and you don't eat them, right?

10. Sex Wax brand surf wax has no other use beyond surfing. Experiment at your own peril.

Left: The array of surfwax options can be daunting. In choosing a wax, simply look at the labels and find the temperature range they are meant for.
Below: Sex Wax brand surf wax has no other use beyond surfing.

The ideal surf spot for beginners is also set apart from places where more experienced surfers reign. Beginners and experienced surfers don't mix: the beginners are usually intimidated and tend to sit on the side and watch. Or they get in the way. Either way, they don't accomplish much.

Thus, the formula is this:

Space + time + gentle waves breaking for a long way over a sandy bottom + warm water + protected from the wind = the ideal beginners surf spot

The problem is, perfect surf spots are rare and perfect beginner waves are rare, too. Around California and the world there are a handful of optimum surf spots that fit this criteria perfectly, including Cowell's Beach in Santa Cruz, Waikiki in Hawaii, Main Beach Noosa in Australia, and Muizenberg in South Africa.

Beginner Surf Beaches

Location, location, location: The best surfing spot for beginners has long, gentle waves breaking for a good distance over a wide, sandy beach.

Surfers wax the deck of their surfboards for traction. Make sure to wax all the way from the nose to the tail.

Lay down a good coat of wax with no bald spots, or you may slip, fall, and embarrass yourself.

WAXING YOUR SURFBOARD

Surf wax smells nice and comes in cool packages with funny names. Unfortunately, surf wax is not needed for Softops. Those boards come with a traction surface that doesn't require wax: "What's nice about the Softop for beginners is you can practice with them on the beach and not worry about sand getting stuck in the wax," surf instructor Carla Rowland says.

Unlike skiers, who use wax on the bottom for speed, surfers use wax on the deck for traction. Learning to surf on a hardboard without wax would be tricky indeed. Some lay a base coat then a top coat, but that's getting fancy.

When Carla surfs, she uses the whole board from the nose to the tail, so she waxes from the nose to the tail. And while she doesn't want to wax her rails and create drag that will slow her down, she waxes where she thinks she might be grabbing the board: "I never know when I might need to grab it and you don't want it slipping from your hands."

Lay down a good coat; no bald spots or you will slip and fall and embarrass yourself. And the smell of surf wax is one of those smells that stays in your smell memory.

Don't wax the surfboard bottom or the fins. Unlike skiing, where you wax for speed, surf wax will only slow you down.

Surf wax is not needed on Softops, as these boards come with a traction surface that doesn't require wax. As Carla says: "What's nice about the Softop for beginners is you can practice with them on the beach and not worry about sand getting stuck in the wax."

SURFBOARD LEASHES

Some blame the surf leash for ruining surfing, inspiring localism, and various other social ills. There was a time when surf spots were divided up by ability, because surfers without leashes who didn't know what they were doing would lose their boards into the rocks and that would be that. Some say localism and fighting over waves took root after surf leashes were popularized in the early 1970s.

Pat O'Neill was one of the first surfers to wear a leash, and when he tried to wear one of the newfangled things at a Malibu surf contest in the 1970s, the other surfers at that event rebelled, snarling things like "Leashes are for dogs!" Despite that cold reception, the leash caught on, and there is some irony in that Jack O'Neill—whose piratey, eye-patched logo adorns all O'Neill wet-suits—lost his eye from a leash accident in the 1970s.

Talk the Talk

Localism is the protection of a particular surf spot by and for local surfers; it can sometimes become territorial or aggressive toward outsiders.

Right A 10-foot-long (3-meter-long) Staycovered leash.
Below: To select a surfboard leash, the equation is simple: "I generally use leashes that are as long as the board I am riding," Carla says. "So for a nine-foot [2.75-meter] longboard, use a nine-foot [2.75-meter] longboard leash."

Different leashes connect to boards in different fashions. Some boards have a piece of material for a loop built in, others require a piece of string or a leash that has loop material. Thread whatever you have through the leash plug, which is usually on the deck of the board. Carla says: "It's important to make sure the leash is fastened tight to the board, because if you lose your board you will have to do the 'rock dance,' and that can include stepping on sea slugs and that is just gross."

Overall, there is no doubt that leashes have made surfing safer. During the 1960s, surfers didn't wear leashes and Malibu was like a logjam of big lumber bashing around and injuring people. The leash made surfing more crowded because it took ability away from the equation, but in general surfing is safer because of it. Especially for beginners.

Carla encourages her students to attach themselves to their surfboards with surf leashes—for their own safety but also for the safety of everyone else in the water. The leash isn't a ticket to let go, however. It is bad form to ever let go of your board and bail in front of other surfers.

But leashes can also be dangerous to their owners. "I call it the **Rubber Band Effect**," Carla explains. "I tell students that they have to remember that strapping a leash to their ankle is like strapping a rubber band to their ankle. When they fall, and the board keeps going, at some point it will return, and they have to watch out for that.

Surfboard Leash Length

Leashes should typically be 4 to 12 inches (10 to 30 centimeters) longer than your board. It is important to have a properly sized leash so that the recoil does not fling the board back at you after you fall.

"I stress this over and over again: Protect your head. When you fall, use your hands to break your fall. And when you surface, surface with your hands protecting your head. I've lost count of the number of times I have been hit by boards that came from nowhere. I have the scars to prove it, and also the memory loss."

Surfboard Leashes

BACK IN THE 1960S, Malibu was as crowded as it is now—maybe more so—but it was a lot more dangerous because no one wore leashes, and loose boards were everywhere. Leashes make surfing safer, I think, although there is always the danger of being hit by your own board when it recoils at the end of a stretched-out leash.

If you look at the O'Neill logo, which is all over Zuma Jay's store, you'll see Jack O'Neill with the eye patch. That eye patch is the result of a leash accident in the 1970s—Jack wiped out, his board came back and hit him and he lost an eye.

Leashes are better now—engineered with materials as high-tech as wetsuits and trunks—but the danger is still there: "We carry four brands of leashes," Zuma Jay said. "For three of the brands we carry everything they make: FCS, Da Kine, and Weapons—which are Larry Block's

private line. Weapons have the longest warranty and the lowest price. We use them on the rentals, because you know how people treat rentals, and they usually last two years—which means they are pretty durable. If I used the high-end FCS or Da Kine leashes on the rentals, people would swap them out. So I don't."

As a rule, the right size leash for a board is the same size as the board, although Jay riffs on that a little: "A seven-foot [2-meter] leash for a seven-foot [2-meter] board is a good rule, although that depends on ability. When I have a seven-foot [2-meter] board I use a six-foot [1¾-meter] leash because modern leashes have six inches [15 centimeters] of rail saver, too. Sometimes for brand-new beginners on an eight-foot [2½-meter] board I will give them a nine-foot [2¾-meter] leash just to get it away from them, because there are some real knuckleheads learning to surf these days."

Leashes strap to your back leg. "Strap it to the ankle, but not too tight," Carla says. "Secure it snugly with the cord on the outside of your ankle. Leashes are useful but they can get underfoot and trip you, and you don't want that."

Surfboard leashes come in many flavors, but the equation is pretty simple: "I generally use leashes that are as long as the board I am riding," Carla says. "So for a nine-foot (2.7-meter) longboard, use a nine-foot (2.7-meter) longboard leash."

Simple as that. But how to attach the leash to the board, and the leash to your ankle?

Different leashes and boards connect differently. Some boards have a piece of material for a loop built in, others require a piece of string, or a leash that has loop material. Thread whatever you have through the **leash plug**, which is usually on the deck of the board—although early leash users would put a hole through the fin and connect the leash there. Not a good idea in terms of drag or safety.

Different leashes fold and seal separately, but it's important to figure it out and get it right.

Carla says: "It's important to make sure the leash is fastened tight to the board, because if you lose your board you will have to do the rock dance and that can include stepping on sea slugs and that is just gross."

Leashes strap to your back leg. "Strap it to the ankle but not too tight," Carla says. "Secure it snugly with the cord on the outside of your ankle. Leashes are useful but they can get you in trouble as well."

PREPARATION

Tan, don't burn: use sunscreen! Even when the sun is not shining, UV rays are making it through space and the atmosphere and onto your skin. Whatever sunscreen you use, it's best to apply it 20 minutes before a session. "Always protect yourself" applies to your skin as well.

Modern wetsuits come with a lot of pockets, straps, hoods, gaskets, seals, and other innovations, so they can be confusing to put on properly. If you're afraid of putting your wetsuit on backwards and looking like a fool, ask a loved one to help you get it right.

Always use sunscreen—even when the sun is not shining. UV rays cut through space and the atmosphere and onto your skin no matter the cloud cover over the ocean.

Getting into your wetsuit with all its pockets, straps, hoods, gaskets, seals, and other innovations can be confusing, exhausting, difficult—or all three. Ask a loved one to help you get it right. Or if you are single, ask a beautiful stranger to help you out.

Carrying Your Surfboard

ALTHOUGH SOFTOP SURFBOARDS are almost indestructible, dragging them on the beach is bad form. And dragging a hardboard is a great way to destroy your expensive investment very quickly. Beginner boards like the Softops are big and wide and hard to carry, but here are the tried and true methods that don't damage the board—or your body.

Carry your surfboard—don't drag it in the sand.

You can carry your board in the crook of your arm, leaning against your shoulder and head. This is the old-school way. When big men with boards weighing 100 pounds (45 kilograms) didn't want to flatten their heads but couldn't get the boards under their arms, they placed them against their heads and made it to the water like he-men.

Carrying your board on your head is acceptable, especially if you do it with style.

FIRST STEPS

After all that preparation, it's time to hit the water. However you approach the water, do it with your head up and your eyes aware and with the knowledge you are now entering an environment that is beautiful and fun, but also always potentially dangerous. Never turn your back on the ocean. Always protect yourself.

"One time I had a little boy about five years old" Carla remembers. "We made it to the water's edge and he said, 'I think I changed my mind.' And that was that. Other times people will be out in the water and give up, and that can be dangerous.

"There was a time when the surf was fairly good and we were out there and in the impact zone when this student just gave up on me. There were waves coming and surfers coming but this person just refused to move. It was dangerous and made me a little mad. Because in surfing there are times when you can't stop and call 'Time out!' You might be tired but there is a set coming and you have to dig deep and get out of trouble. Or you're gonna get beat to hell."

Talk the Talk

The **shorebreak** is where the ocean meets the land.

The area where the ocean meets the land is called the **shorebreak**. Depending on the size of the surf, this area can be benign or dangerous. Surfing requires patience and knowledge, and here is a good place to practice patience. If there are waves breaking, wait them out; wait for a calm period, then hit the water, and paddle, paddle, paddle.

Carla is a believer in what she calls "dry hair sessions:" "I like to get my students off the beach, through the shorebreak, and out the back with dry hair. So I teach them patience and timing. While standing on the beach, getting ready to paddle out, watch the ocean, study it: How far apart are the sets? How many waves are there in a set? How is the crowd? As you are waiting, study the conditions, then shove off. Making it out the back with dry hair is the way to go."

Carla encourages people to get directly onto their feet as fast as possible. But some people are more comfortable riding on their knees until they are stable and then getting to their feet: "Riding on the knees can develop a bad habit," Carla believes. "Being dependent on that position in order to get up can make the standup process take a little longer."

Surfing is all about patience: paddling, waiting for the right wave, paddling again to catch it, popping up, wiping out—and then doing it all over again.

"There are very few people who get up and do it on the first wave," Carla explains. "There are remarkable people who do that, though. Surfing isn't like throwing a baseball. It's not something you learn in an hour or two. Surfing is something you pick up over years."

The shorebreak is the point where the ocean meets land—and if the surf is big, the shorebreak can be dangerous. If there are big waves breaking, wait.

Hit the water when you have a calm period between breaking waves.

Talk the Talk

The **lineup area** is where surfers wait for waves and is located outside of the break.

Surfing is all about patience. You'll often have a long wait for the perfect wave. Sit outside where the waves break in what's called the lineup area.

Waiting for waves, surfers often lay prone in the paddling position. But you can also sit upright so you can see the waves coming into view.

Talk the Talk

A **buoy** is a derogatory term for a surfer who sits in the lineup without catching waves.

When you pick your wave, paddle, paddle, paddle.

As the wave begins to break on the tail of your board, get set to pop up.

As you practiced on the beach, pop up with speed, determination, and strength.

Successfully getting to your feet is all about balance.

Paddling with the wave, you can feel with your feet when it begins to break.

Push yourself quickly upwards as the wave breaks around the tail of your board.

Being in the correct paddling position—your chest up and lower back arched—will greatly help you in the transition from prone to standing.

When you pop up, you need your feet underneath you as quickly as possible; use your upper-body strength to move fast.

You need to be quick as well in getting your balance on your feet.

Your arms will no longer be your paddles; now, you'll rely on them to balance your upper body.

Keep your knees bent to get your balance and assure your stability.

The moment of truth. The proper position, as here, is in the middle of the board, with long, smooth strokes, swiveling your head to see where the wave is forming.

If your weight is a little too far forward and at an angle, as here, your board will dig into the water and pearl.

If you feel yourself starting to pearl, quickly shift your weight backward to rescue yourself.

Popping up and standing is a fine art that's all about speed and balance.

The waves will quickly teach you when you don't have things just right.

Training Kate

**SURF INSTRUCTOR JOHN PHILBIN
TRANSFORMS KATE BOSWORTH INTO
A SURFER GIRL FOR *BLUE CRUSH***

BY JOHN PHILBIN WITH BEN MARCUS

Many actors and actresses have played surfers over the years. It's a long list of names, including icons and Oscar winners like Sandra Dee, Elvis Presley, Cliff Robertson, Jan Michael Vincent, Patrick Swayze, Gary Busey, Keanu Reeves, and Cameron Diaz. Of all them, Kate Bosworth looked the most natural on a surfboard and in the water. And that's largely thanks to surf instructor John Philbin, who taught her to ride waves.

In the 2002 Hollywood film *Blue Crush*, Kate portrayed Anne Marie Chadwick, a *haole* who struggles to overcome fears from a past wipeout to compete at a gnarly Pipeline contest.

Talk the Talk

Adapted from an ancient Hawaiian term of greeting, a **haole** is a local Hawaiian surfer.

Banzai Pipeline is a monster wave on the North Shore of Oahu, Hawaii. It's commonly known as **Pipe** due to the perfect, hollow tube shape of the breaking wave.

Glasser is short for a "fiberglasser"— someone who makes surfboards.

Early on in the movie, there is a shot of a young, blonde surfer girl paddling out at Pipeline. It's a big day there: surfers and bodyboarders are dropping in, some are getting barreled, some are wiping out. And there is Anne Marie paddling into the middle of it all. In most movies, paddling out into 10-foot (3-meter) Pipeline waves would be considered too hazardous for an actor or actress to do themselves, so the actual paddling would be done by a stunt double. But in this scene, you don't have to look too close to realize that the girl paddling out at Pipeline really is Kate. She looks *real*.

You may ask yourself: "How did she get there?"

IN JOHN'S HANDS

John Philbin helped put Kate there in the danger at Pipeline. Growing up as a surfer in Palos Verdes, California, John dreamed of surfing Pipeline and acting in movies. He earned a degree in theater from the University of Southern California then studied at the Loft Studio with Sean Penn, Nicholas Cage, Meg Ryan, Michelle Pfeiffer, Laura Dern, and Eric Stoltz, among many others. Sometimes dreams come true, and John's dreams came together when he got to surf Pipeline in front of the camera for two movies: In Universal's 1987 cult classic *The North Shore*, Philbin nailed the role of Turtle, a transplanted *haole* glasser with a pidgin accent thicker than the resin he spread on surfboards. Four years later, Philbin was the bank robber in the Jimmy Carter mask in *Point Break*. Most recently, Philbin played a villain again in Brian Grazer's TV pilot *The Break*, which was directed by John Stockwell, starred Kala Alexander, and employed the exact same water safety team as *Blue Crush*.

With those credits on his resume, combined with his experience as a surfer, John has been teaching surfing professionally since 1999. He teaches the famous and the anonymous—anyone who wants to learn—and sometimes works with feature film and television productions whenever authenticity and the integrity of the production are desired.

Philbin was hired for *Blue Crush* by John Stockwell. The film was produced by Brian Grazer, one of the co-founders of Imagine Films; Grazer's movies, like *Splash* and *Eight Mile* and *A Beautiful Mind*, have been nominated for more Academy Awards than surfer Kelly Slater has won World Titles. Grazer and Stockwell are two guys who would rather get caught inside at 15-foot (14.6-meter) Sunset then make a sloppy movie, and the success of *Blue Crush* depended on transforming their actress into a believable surfer.

MAKING ANNE MARIE

In summer 2001, Kate Bosworth was 19 years old and fresh out of high school in Connecticut, where she had been a National Merit Scholar. Princeton had accepted her but she deferred her entrance to have a go at Hollywood. By summer 2001, Bosworth had four roles to her credit, mostly small parts in the movies *The Horse Whisperer*, *The Newcomers*, and *Remember the Titans*, and a role in the *Young Americans* TV show.

Actress/surfer Kate Bosworth and surfer/actor John Philbin on the beach at Malibu, training for Bosworth's role as Mary Anne Chadwick in *Blue Crush. Courtesy John Philbin*

Bosworth was ambitious and determined, a young, blonde actress with talent in an extremely competitive business loaded with young, blonde, talented actresses. Now she was up for a starring role in a Brian Grazer movie, and in true Hollywood fashion, she was smart enough not to talk her way out of the role: "Kate was not entirely truthful about having surfing experience when we talked to her about the role," Stockwell says. "So she quickly went out and took surf lessons before the surf audition."

Kate met her surf instructor John Philbin at the Cross Creek Starbucks in Malibu, less than a mile (1.6 kilometers) from the surfbreak at First Point. "Kate was on time and enthusiastic," Philbin says. "At first impression she was very athletic and beautiful. I could see right away why they were interested in her for the role—but she couldn't surf. My job was to get her in the water and see if she had what it would take to realistically portray a surfer on Hawaii's North Shore."

It was Philbin's job to show Bosworth how to walk the walk, talk the talk, paddle, catch waves, and make it look

natural. From Sandra Dee in *Gidget* to Cameron Diaz in *Charlie's Angels III*, most actors and actresses have had trouble looking like surfers, and one of the dead giveaways is paddling. "Paddling in the ocean may not sound so very glamorous but surfing is 90 percent paddling," John says. "I teach that position is everything in the ocean, and paddling is how you get there. Paddling is how you catch a wave and how you get away from one. You paddle to get out of danger or closer to it. The difference between relative safety in the ocean and extreme peril is often a few more paddles. Especially at the location her character was supposed to surf: the Banzai Pipeline."

PIPELINE ISSUES

In *Blue Crush*, Anne Marie Chadwick is an experienced pro surfer with Pipeline issues. She is afraid of the spot, her fears fortified by an unfading memory of wiping out there, cracking her head on the bottom, and nearly drowning. Because Pipeline was the stage for *Blue Crush*, Kate would not only have to look natural on a surfboard, she would have to do it within 50 yards (46 meters) of one of the most dangerous surf spots on earth.

Kate wasn't expected to surf Pipeline. Her surfing would be doubled by Rochelle Ballard and Noah Johnson. But she had to be ready for her close-ups, and that meant paddling and duck diving and moving through the ocean like a real surfer girl. "I knew that Kate would have to be able to paddle and sit stable and do dialogue over and over again," John says. "But I knew she had what it would take after our very first lesson. Kate is a natural athlete. Most movie stars are, because it's a very physical job. The gentle waves of Malibu provided the perfect opportunities for her to practice beginning surfing skills. She showed up on time, followed my directions, stood up, rode a wave, and showed the first sign of some talent in the water. Kate was determined to get it right—get it perfect. I was being paid by the producers and part of my job was to report on her progress truthfully to the producer and director each day. What they were looking for was determination, willingness, a certain athleticism, and bravery. Surfing is not for everyone. It's hard and it can be scary."

Training Kate meant a lot of hours in the ocean, two to four hours a day, four to six days a week, an intense immersion—so to speak—into this strange new world of ocean, waves, and how to catch them. "The situations and choices presented any surfer in the water and on land are unique, varied and infinite," John says. "The situation is always fluid, so I trained Kate how to go with the flow. We would start our sessions checking the forecast. We were going out anyway but it was interesting comparing notes. Then we'd drive to whatever spot we thought would be best for what we were working on.

"We would observe our surf spots at different tides and learn how the ocean bottom forms the waves. We studied how the white water revealed the shape of the reefs, rocks, and channels. We mapped out lineups. We worked on the basics, over and over and over again: Taking the boards off the car and putting them back on, waxing the boards, attaching and detaching leashes, putting in fins, carrying the boards long distances. The board was a prop and a tool, and familiarity was king.

"We entered and exited the water over and over and over again. I usually tell students that this is the most dangerous part of surfing and to treat this boundary—where the water meets the land—with the utmost respect; as almost a religious observance."

And when there was no surf, they paddled: "Through waves, over waves, under waves," John says. "I knew duck diving would be important so we drilled 100 duck dives into a long-distance paddle. When waves graced our sessions we'd practice catching them. Making a commitment to catch a wave: This is what usually separates respected surfers from all the rest. It is a quality that is very hard to teach.

"Usually you just hear a surf instructor screaming 'Paddle, paddle, paddle!' I was out at Waimea Bay the other day while Kelly Slater was giving his brother and Jon Jon Florence a lesson on where to sit and how to catch a good one at the Bay. 'Go, go, go!' were his words of choice. But in order to 'go' you've got to 'paddle!' And we mean paddle hard, harder—paddle as hard and as fast as you can. Paddle as if your life depended on it, because someday it might. With moms I change it to: Paddle as if the life of your child were at stake."

Blue Crush ends with a climactic, two-woman heat at the Pipe Masters. Anne Marie has done well enough to make it to the final, where she meets real surfer Keala Kennelly and faces her fears in big, gnarly, 10-foot (3-meter) Pipe. After wiping out, Anne Marie is sitting on the shoulder, afraid to paddle back into the pit when she is confronted by Kennelly: "What are you doing?" Kennelly says, then guides her opponent back into the peak where Chadwick snags a perfect wave.

It's a nice ending—and a true ending—because one thing Bosworth learned about this strange, new surfing world is the camaraderie shared by everyone paddling around on pieces of plastic.

ADVICE FROM LAIRD HAMILTON

The art of the movie was Kate's reality while doing a session at Point Dume: "Laird Hamilton came by doing his stand up paddle thing," Philbin says. "And offered Kate one tip. He suggested she stand up quickly, as soon as she could, as soon as she caught the wave. Who's gonna argue with Laird?

"But he had a point. We are all more coordinated standing on our feet than in any other position. So it makes sense to get to our feet as soon as possible.

"Pop up drills, by the way, are the only drills we can practice on land that really come in handy in the water. I first use a line in the sand, across which both feet straddle, then a narrow park bench. If you can stand up between your hands and under your body on a narrow bench you can do it on a board."

ALWAYS PROTECT YOURSELF

John Philbin has taught hundreds of beginners to surf, but Kate was a little different because there was a $30 million movie resting on her shoulders—which were getting muscular and strong from all the paddling. While teaching Kate, Philbin had to be sure she was safe in the ocean, because an injury could have lead to Kate losing the part or delaying the start of shooting: "I stressed safety in all of our sessions, and the number-one thing I stressed with Kate—as I do with all my students is simple: protect your head. Surfing is statistically safer than cheerleading. Certainly safer than riding a bike or jumping a horse or snowboarding or skateboarding, because when you fall, it's only water. Unless you hit something hard.

"The number-one cause of injury in surfing is head trauma caused by your own board. If you can eliminate this, you may never get injured surfing. Always protect your head from your own board—with your hands or a helmet. If you lose control of your board, assume it's gonna come back and hit you in the head. This way, if it ever does, you're ready for it and can prevent any serious impact.

"The other hard object is the ocean bottom. No head-first diving or feet-first jumping, try not to penetrate to the bottom. Fall flat or dive shallow, and protect your head. Last but not least: other people and their boards. Tamayo Perry learned that the hard way at Pipeline and almost lost his scalp, but getting hit by someone else's board is a danger from the beginner's spot at the end of Sunset Boulevard in Los Angeles to the triple black diamond Sunset Beach in Hawaii."

THE BIG BREAK

Philbin trained Kate for a solid month, four to six days a week, and while he wanted to see his young apprentice do well and get the part, he also had to be honest with the producers and director: "Through the fourth week of training I was responsible for calling the line producer Rick Delago and director John Stockwell every day to report on Kate's progress and learning curve—what skills she was acquiring and her determination. While we were swirling around in the ocean, back in Hollywood there was a swirl of decisions about looks, money, studio approval, and the director's belief in the actor's talent for the role."

Blue Crush, and the part of Anne Marie, was a big deal for Kate. It is a miracle when any actor gets any role because of all the competition, but a starring role in a Brian Grazer movie had the potential to launch Kate as a movie star. The part of a lifetime, really, for a young Hollywood hopeful: "Kate got the job after the fourth week, and we were both stoked," Philbin says. "Kate's dedication to the training had really paid off and it was rewarding for me to help a young actress get her break. She continued to suit up and show up for another two weeks before she flew off to Hawaii and into the capable care of Brian Keaulana and Brock Little—the most respected big-wave ocean safety team in the world."

As Kate whirled off to Hawaii for a graduate course in Hawaiian power, Philbin stayed behind in California, wondering how his young apprentice was doing on the North Shore: "I did not see Kate for quite a while. After our introduction to the ocean in California, Kate got pulled into the big time in Hawaii. I heard that Brock Little took her into the shorebreak at Waimea to give her a taste of Hawaiian power, and I heard she did great.

"Four weeks after I handed her off to Brock and Brian—and ten weeks after she had taken those first small steps at Malibu—I flew to Hawaii to visit the set. Kate showed me some dailies of her paddling out into the lineup, at ten-foot [3-meter] Pipeline. That same footage made it into the movie, and when I first saw it I was shocked. At first I thought it was fake, or someone was doubling for Kate. I watched the scene over and over again, and freeze-framed it and still I was incredulous. But there she was, no question, that pale equestrienne from Connecticut was now a tanned, determined surfer girl. Her back muscles were ripped and rippling as she paddled out into the lineup at ten-foot [3-meter] Pipeline. These were life threatening conditions, but she looked powerful and focused and, most importantly, completely natural as the awesome Pipeline bombs exploded on the shallow reef beside her.

"The one thing I noticed most of all: she was paddling hard."

chapter 6

Learning the Secrets of the Sea

THE OCEAN IS DANGEROUS; it is mysterious. A good part of the attraction to surfing is the total immersion—so to speak—in this foreign environment, a place where humans are not entirely comfortable, where we are not even the apex predator.

The poet Henry Wadsworth Longfellow wrote of the ocean,

Woulds't thou, so the helmsman answered
Learn the secrets of the sea?
Only those who brave its danger comprehend its mystery.

Left: When the surf's calm, the ocean's famous for another facet of its beauty. *Right:* When the surf's up, the waves can be big and beautiful—as well as dangerous. *Epic Stock/Shutterstock.*

Understanding the secrets of the sea was the lifeblood of the Hawaiians who pioneered surfriding. This engraving from 1878 shows "Surf Swimming by Sandwich Islanders" from the Reverend J. G. Wood's *The Uncivilized Races of Man in All Countries of the World*.

The only way to comprehend the mysteries of the sea may be to brave its dangers, but comprehending its mysteries will become a lifelong learning experience, bordering on obsession.

WAVE TYPES AND FORMATION

Most surfing waves are formed by wind blowing over the water. That energy moving through the ocean organizes itself into **swells**. Those swells then **break** as waves when they feel the friction of the ocean bottom as they approach the coast.

But there are exceptions.

In the Amazon basin of Brazil, the Severn River of England, Alaska's Turnagain Arm, and about a half dozen other locations around the world, surfers will ride waves called **tidal bores** for many miles up rivers and estuaries. Tidal bores are a phenomenon caused where a narrowing of the land mass around a body of water causes the incoming tide to appear as a breaking wave. It's an interesting phenomenon, but something for the most experienced surfers.

In August 2007, Hawaiian extreme surfers Garrett McNamara and Keali'i Mamala used personal watercraft to tow into waves formed by

Pipeline is one of the most famous surf spots in the world. The wave breaks over a reef on the North Shore of Oahu, Hawaii. *Lucia Griggi*

massive pieces of ice calving from the fronts of glaciers. Even the most experienced surfers aren't interested in riding these waves, and Gmac and Keali'i are just a little nuts.

Tsunami waves are formed by massive movements of earth displacing massive amounts of water. Looking at the video of the infamous Indian Ocean tsunami of 2004: there were instances where those waves could have been ridden by surfers, but that would have been very lucky (or unlucky) and brave surfers to have been in the right place at the right time to catch those once in a lifetime (hopefully) waves when they came through.

Finally, there are **artificial waves** generated in wave pools around the world.

Still, for 99.9 percent of all beginning surfers, the first waves they ride will be **surface ocean waves** generated by the wind—energy that has traveled a short or great distance through deep water in the form of swells. When those swells approach shallow water, their energy is forced upward until gravity topples it over and forms waves.

THE SCIENCE OF SURFABLE WAVES

A "calm" ocean, according to the maritime guiding Beaufort Scale, has no wind blowing at all. This is maybe good for local surfing conditions when the waves finally arrive, but without wind, there are no capillary waves, then ripples, then wavelets to form a sea, no sea to form a swell, and no swell to break into waves.

Wind blowing across the surface of the ocean transfers energy that forms **ripples**, which fan out at 70- to 80-degree angles from the direction of the wind. As the ripples get larger and the wind continues

Opposite: Some of the biggest surfing waves in the world strike France's Atlantic Coast. Here, pro surfer Celine Gerhart carves a bottom turn at Hossegor, France. *Lucia Griggi*

to blow on the backs of the ripples, they become larger, called **wavelets**. If the wind continues to blow and more wavelets are formed, at some point that becomes a **sea**, which is an area of water effected by the wind. The energy in a sea is chaotic, and in a fully developed sea, wavelets of various sizes and wavelengths react and interact, some wavelets canceling each other but others combining their energy in one direction, to become a **swell**. A swell is a train of waves of similar wavelengths, moving across the ocean in the same direction.

Fetch is the term for the length of ocean over which wind blows. When you combine wind speed and wind duration over fetch length, that equation adds up to the size and energy and quality of a swell.

In any sea there are swells with differing **wavelengths**, or the distance between swell crests, based on how long the wind has been blowing and in what direction. Short-period swells are newer and they begin to die as the energy moves out of the area of blowing wind. Swells that were produced earlier in the storm have the energy to continue moving through the ocean. And like ripples from a very large pebble thrown into a very large pool of water, these swells have the energy to continue without the influence of the wind.

By the time a swell has moved 800 nautical miles (1,500 kilometers) away from the wind source, it has lost almost two-thirds of its size, with the shorter-period energy fading away. Swells move through the ocean with a speed that is a factor of their wavelength. Swells with longer wave crests move faster than those with shorter wave crests, and one of the phenomena of swells moving through open ocean is that swells with similar wavelengths will group together.

A sea is a mass of energy with a wavelength of less than 10 seconds, while a swell is anything over 10 seconds. As you become a more experienced surfer, you will learn to live and die by not just the size of a predicted swell, but also the **period**, because the period is an indication of the power and speed of the swell. Maverick's surfers get all excited when a 20-foot (6-meter) swell approaches with a period of 20 seconds or over, because this tells them that the swell has moved a long way through the ocean and will arrive over the reef in the form of big, orderly, powerful waves.

Talk the Talk

Maverick's is a famous—or more correctly, an infamous—surfing break located one-half mile (800 meters) off the coast of Half Moon Bay, California.

Mark Sponsler is a Maverick's surfer and dedicated surf predictor who is one of the first to deliver the good news when a swell approaches the northern California coast at 20 seconds or more: "A forty- to forty-five-foot [12- to 14-meter] sea can generate a twenty-plus-second period swell assuming the swell has sufficient distance to **unwrap**, and by that I mean the distance that raw, untamed waves generated under the influence of wind must travel away from that fetch before they settle down into regular, well-spaced swells," he explains. "It's sort of like 'unwrapping' a Christmas present by peeling off the outer papers to expose the gem hidden inside.

"Unwrapping normally takes about twelve hundred nautical miles [2,200 kilometers]. In other words you don't want the swell-generating storm to get closer to your shore than that distance."

Swells with longer periods move better and longer through the ocean, because longer-period swells carry more energy with them. And because the wavelength is stretched out and longer, the wave peaks are not as high and defined, and are less prone to decay from winds and contrary currents and other swells.

A **wave train** is a group of swells of similar wavelengths. Their dynamics are also a natural phenomenon, as they move through the ocean like a pack of bicyclists: the lead swell in a wave train eventually slows down and moves to the rear of the wave train, while swells in the rear with more energy move to the front.

The speed of a swell through the open ocean is the period of the wave multiplied by 1.5, so the speed of an 18-second period swell is 28 nautical miles per hour (51.8 kilometers per hour), or 33.6 miles per hour (54 kilometers per hour). That equation works for the open ocean, when all that energy is moving through very deep water and is feeling no friction from the ocean bottom. That equation changes when an open ocean swell approaches the continental shelf of major land masses or when it suddenly trips over reefs that rise abruptly around tropical islands.

When wave trains move out of the open ocean and enter shallower waters, their period again is a factor, as period relates directly to wavelength, and wavelength relates to the speed of a wave train in relation to the depth of the water.

Waves begin to feel the ocean bottom at one-half of the wavelength. Doing the math for an 18-second swell, 18 squared is 324, and that multiplied by 2.56 is 829 feet (253 meters), so a swell train with a period of 18 seconds begins to feel the bottom in about 800 feet (244 meters) of water. Large continents usually have a continental shelf that extends for hundreds of miles from the coast, while surf spots in the open ocean sometimes have no shelf at all, which is why waves like Teahupoo and Pipeline and Jaws break with such power.

Shoaling is a phenomenon that occurs when an open ocean swell approaches shore, begins to feel the bottom, and the friction slows things down. As the water depth gets shallower, the energy stored in the base of a swell is pushed upward and the wave height increases.

Surfers who know how to do the math look for period as much as wave height when a swell approaches the coast, because a 5-foot (1½-meter) wave with a 12-second period will not be as big as a 4-foot (1¼-meter) swell with a 20-second period.

Also, a long-period swell will "shoal," or feel the bottom and "wrap" into a coast, sooner than will a short-period swell, and that wrapping effect brings the swell into areas of the coast that a shorter-period swell will miss.

Local conditions also have a lot to do with how waves are when they finally arrive: Tides, currents, local winds, and cloud conditions put the final icing on the cake of a swell, and that icing can be sweet or sour. A tide that is too high or too low will leave too much water on the reef, or not enough, and that will spoil the effect.

Talk the Talk

Teahupoo is a world-renowned surfing spot off Tahiti, in French Polynesia in the southern Pacific Ocean. It's famed for its hollow, powerful waves, often reaching 7 to 10 feet (2 to 3 meters) and higher.

Jaws is a big-wave surfing reef break on the island of Maui, Hawaii. It's called Jaws due to the size and ferocity of the waves, which can reach heights of 70 feet (21 meters).

Big-wave surfing is the domain of a crazy few of the world's best surfers. To catch such monstrous waves, surfers are usually towed into them behind personal watercraft, since the waves move too fast for humans to paddle into. *Shutterstock*

HOW TO SPOT GOOD SURFING WAVES

When open ocean swells approach a coastline, their final moments are affected by many factors: the depth of the ocean bottom, local tides, local currents, winds, and the last few hundred yards (meters) of ocean before it becomes dry land.

Using the Malibu coast as an example, to the northwest, Zuma Beach is a **beachbreak**—a long expanse of sand with a bottom contour that is constantly shape-shifting due to currents, tides, and season. As swells approach Zuma Beach, they encounter high and low spots in the bottom contour, also based on the shape of sandbars and the height of the tide. Surfers looking at Zuma Beach will see sandbars and channels. A practiced eye can gauge where the approaching swell will form good waves for surfing—waves with a peak breaking to the right or the left, or both ways.

South of Zuma, Point Dume has two point breaks—at Big Dume and Little Dume. The phenomenon here is called **refraction**, where the swell moving along a point of land will slow down where it feels shallow water, but the rest of the wave will continue moving, or **wrapping**, into the point. Point waves are generally the favored kind of wave for most surfers, as refraction causes a long, breaking wall to form and fall evenly.

Around Point Dume there are also reefs outside the point where waves break on the bigger days. The reef comes abruptly out of the ocean and is surrounded on both sides by deeper water, so the incoming swells break in a peak, allowing surfers to ride right or left. On the really good days at Point Dume, the outside peak will break and move into the point, allowing surfers to get a thrilling takeoff on the outside, then move onto the point for a long ride into the beach.

Moving down the coast, Malibu has a number of smaller beachbreaks, points, and reefs that are not as popular as Zuma Beach or Point Dume, but which all have their good days based on the size, angle, and period of the swell, and also local winds and tides.

In the middle of Malibu, Surfrider Beach is a classic California point break made of sand, cobblestones, and other debris washed down from the mountains by Malibu Creek. Over the centuries and millennia, the creek washing out and the ocean washing in have formed that sandbar into a perfect receptacle for ocean swells approaching the coast from the south, southwest, and west.

Malibu is a classic **point break**, where waves will start breaking at the rivermouth, or Third Point, and then move through Second Point and First Point and toward the Malibu Pier. There are movies of Malibu, shot in 1947, that show the entire point connecting in one long wave from Third Point to past the front of the pier. Changes in sand flow caused by coastal construction, and changes in the shape of Malibu Creek, have changed the shape of the point, and it doesn't "connect" like that anymore, which is a shame.

On the inside of First Point, the Malibu Pier itself is not a surf spot, although on the biggest days, some daring surfers will ride swells through the pilings and to the other side. In other parts of California, like Huntington Beach and Newport and Mission Beach and Santa Barbara, man-made obstructions like piers and jetties will stop sand flow and form sandbars that create good waves for surfing. Some of the best waves in California are there because humans messed with Mother Nature: The Newport Wedge, the Huntington Pier, Sandspit at the Santa Barbara harbor mouth, and dozens of **jetty breaks** and **pier breaks** from Coronado to Crescent City.

CONDITIONS: TIDE, WIND, CURRENTS

When surfers look at a beachbreak, point, reef, jetty, or a pier break, they will look at how the swell is approaching first, but then they will also look at the conditions, which means how the local tide and winds and even sunlight and clouds are affecting the waves.

Tides are massive ocean currents effected by the gravitational push of the sun and moon. While the gravitational effect of the sun is many times more massive than the moon, the moon is closer and so it is the moon that effects local tides more.

Some surfers seem to have the local tides memorized and calculated in an internal clock, while the rest of us have to refer to tide charts that are available online, in local newspapers, or in tide charts posted on lifeguard towers or handed out in local surf shops and fishing stores.

Some surfers like higher tides, some like lower, and tide affects every individual surf spot in its own way. Some **mysto breaks** won't start breaking until the low tide is in the negatives, while other spots completely shut down when the tide goes too low, or too high.

In general, a low tide rising to a higher tide is best for surfing, as an outgoing tide tends to work against an incoming swell, while an incoming tide sweeps that energy in with it.

Because First Point Malibu is a point break with a rocky bottom, low tides sometimes stretch the wave out and cause **sections** in the wave that make it harder or impossible to ride from the top to the bottom. Malibu is generally best on a tide that is rising from low to high.

Malibu surfers are all too familiar with a local phenomenon called **tidacid**, where a too-low or too-high tide will effectively shut off the waves for a period of an hour or more as the tide cycles through its highs or lows.

There are other surf spots around Malibu that only break on very low tides, like the waves that break along the points in front of the popular restaurants at Dukes and Chart House.

Appreciating tides and how they affect the break you are surfing is all part of the learning curve of understanding how to surf. In general, waves are made of water, so the more water the better, but that is not always true.

Talk the Talk

A **mysto break** is an elusive break that only turns into a surfable wave—or **fires**—on rare occasions under specific conditions.

THE EFFECTS OF OFFSHORE AND ONSHORE WINDS

Local winds blowing along a surf spot affect wave conditions as much or more than tide. Contrary winds can destroy a surf session and send everyone home depressed, while favorable winds can turn average waves into exceptional waves.

Glossary of Ocean Terms

A-frame: Another expression for a peak—a wave breaking right and left with perfect shape.

Artificial reef: Over the years there have been several attempts to lay down materials to create artificial reefs for surfing. They have all been unsuccessful, while at the same time, humans are geniuses at creating rideable waves by accident.

Backdoor: When a surfer pulls into a hollow section from behind the section, that is known as backdooring the section.

Back off: When a wave starts to break in shallow water and then moves into deep water, it backs off and becomes less steep and hollow.

Backwash: When wave energy sweeps up the beach it returns to sea in the form of backwash, which can sometimes collide with incoming waves and create explosions of water.

Barrel: Another expression for the breaking part of the wave, also known as the **curl** or **tube**.

Beachbreak: Waves that break over sandbars on a stretch of beach.

Blown out: An undesirable condition, when contrary waves blow over the tops of incoming waves, crumbling the curl and creating sections along the wave, making them difficult to ride.

Bluebird: A Hawaiian expression for big, long, beautiful, blue waves breaking way out to sea.

Bomb: A wave that is bigger than others on a given day. There can also be a **bomb set** of waves that is bigger than the rest.

Bombora: An Australian expression for an outer reef—a wave breaking as far as a mile (1.6 kilometers) out to sea, in deep water surrounded by deeper water.

Bottom: The floor of the ocean, which can be sand, rock, lava, coral, or any combination of those elements.

Bowl: A hollow part of a wave that is feeling the ocean bottom.

Breaking: What a wave does when it's feeling the ocean bottom and friction and gravity topple the swell energy forward.

Break line: Also called the **surfline** or **impact zone**— the part of a surf spot where waves break along a shallow reef.

Broken up: An incoming swell can be cut up by wind and currents and other swells, and that breaks up the even lines. That can be good for beachbreaks, but not as good for reefs and points.

Bumpy: A usually undesirable condition in which onshore winds, backwash, or currents create lumps in the wave face.

Capping: When incoming waves start to foam at the top as they feel bottom, but don't break.

Choppy: A usually undesirable condition in which onshore winds, backwash, or currents create lumps in the wave face.

Clean: A desirable condition in which good waves are complemented by favorable winds, the right tide, and overall good conditions.

Clean-up set: A set of waves that is bigger than the others, which breaks farther out and "cleans up" all the surfers sitting in what was the regular lineup for that day. Clean-up sets happen on rising swells, but they can also come at any time, because the ocean is like a box of chocolates—you never know what is coming next.

Closeout: An undesirable situation, when a wave breaks all at once with no shape or shoulder, leaving a surfer nowhere to go but to the bottom.

A surfer rides the breaking crest of a wave as it curls away behind him. *Nicholas Rjabow/Shutterstock*

Cloud break: Similar to a **bombora**—a wave breaking as much as a mile (1.6 kilometers) out to sea.

Combo swell: Swells can come in from multiple directions at the same time, creating a combo swell.

Consistent: A desirable condition where a swell has a lot of sets and a lot of waves in the set.

Continental shelf: An area of a land mass extending out to sea, sometimes for hundreds of miles. The continental shelf creates drag that slows waves approaching continents. Island waves do not have a continental shelf, and that is why the waves of Hawaii and Teahupoo are so powerful.

Corduroy: When a big, even, lined-up swell is moving toward shore, surfers get all poetic and describe it as "corduroy to the horizon."

Corners: An expression for the rideable parts of a wave.

Crest: The top of the wave. Waves are sometimes measured from trough to crest.

Cross chop: A usually undesirable condition, when unfavorable winds or currents flow bumps or chops into the wave face and create sections that crumble ahead of the curl line.

Curl: The original surfer expression for the breaking part of the wave as it falls forward. "Shooting the curl" is what surfers in the 1950s and 1960s called what modern surfers call "getting shacked" or "getting barreled."

Current: A flow of water created by winds, tides, or channels in the reef. Some currents are favorable and can be used to paddle out to the surf zone. Some currents are unfavorable and can drown you.

Cyclone: An area of closed, circular fluid motion rotating in the same direction as the earth. Usually centered on areas of low atmospheric pressure, cyclones can be wave machines that produce the kinds of long, perfect waves seen at Superbank in Queensland, Australia, and along the reefs of Indonesia.

Cylinder: Another expression for the tube, when a curling wave resembles a hollow cylinder.

Deep water breaks: There are reefs and sandbars far offshore surrounded by deep water, where incoming swells will break. The king daddy deep water break of them all is the Cortes Bank, 100 miles (160 kilometers) out to sea from the Mexico–California border.

Degrees: The compass is divided into 360 degrees, because that number is divisible by 1, 2, 3, 4, 6, and 9. Swell forecasters measure incoming swells by the degree of compass they are approaching from. Local surfers learn which directions are favorable.

Direction: Swells will approach a surf spot from all points of the compass, and "direction" refers to the angle they are coming from.

Double up: When a bigger wave overcomes a smaller wave, the wave face "doubles up" into two breaking waves. Sometimes this is favorable; sometimes it's disastrous.

Down the line: A "down the line" wave is a fast wave with a long wall that requires speed and skill.

Drop: The start of the wave, after paddling in and getting to your feet and before the first turn.

Dumping: An unfavorable condition, similar to a **closeout**, in which a wave breaks all at once, leaving nowhere for a surfer to go.

Duration: Same as wavelength: the period between wave crests as measured in seconds.

Face: The front of the wave, from trough to crest. Some surfers measure waves by the height of the face, some by the back.

Face height: Some surfers measure waves from the back, some from the front. A fair measurement is to measure by body height, as in an ankle slapper, head-high, overhead, or double overhead.

Feathering: Similar to **capping**. When big waves approach and start to feel the reef, they will feather at the top, putting up little spouts of whitewater and foam. Surfers use feathering waves to line up on big days.

Fetch: A length of ocean over which wind blows, to create swells. The longer the fetch and the greater the winds, the greater amount of energy is imparted to the ocean.

Firing: A favorable condition, in which good-quality waves are breaking consistently.

Flat: An undesirable condition of no surf.

Foam: The whitewater created by a broken wave.

Glassy: A favorable condition in which there is no wind to ripple the wave face.

Gnarly: Can be a favorable or an unfavorable condition in which waves are powerful, dangerous, or difficult to ride.

Going off: Similar to **firing**: a favorable condition when all conditions are go—swell, wind, and tide—and the waves are clean and consistent.

Groundswell: Kind of a misleading term, because this has nothing to do with ground. A groundswell is a fully unwrapped swell that has traveled thousands of miles through the ocean, has a period/wavelength of 15 seconds or more, and is lined up and powerful.

Hollow: A wave breaking over a shallow bottom, forming an open area in the curl or tube.

Hurricane: A tropical cyclone with winds greater than 74 miles per hour (200 kilometers per hour). Hurricanes are responsible for great surf on the East Coast of the United States, but also incredible damage. Pacific hurricanes off the Baja peninsula also create surf for the West Coast.

Impact zone: The area where surf is breaking. The point of impact with the lip and the trough and then the foamy area inside that.

Inconsistent: An unfavorable condition where sets of waves are many minutes—or hours—apart and there aren't many waves in a set.

Inside: As opposed to **outside:** the inside of a break is where the waves end and is also the impact zone.

Interval: Same as **swell period**.

Jacking: When a wave hits a shallow bottom suddenly, the lip rears up and throws forward abruptly.

Left: As seen from shore, a wave that is breaking to your right. As seen while paddling into a wave, a wave that is breaking to your left. Pipeline; the Wedge in Newport Beach, California; Seaside in Oregon; and Unstad in Norway are all famous lefts.

Lined up: A favorable condition, when waves break with a long wall and an evenly falling curl.

Lines: What surfers call incoming swell—and the more the merrier.

Lineup: The area of a surfbreak that is the ideal take-off spot. The lineup changes with swell direction, tide, and wind. Experienced surfers will figure out a lineup from day to day and triangulate their position using landforms and/or stationary objects offshore to stay in the proper spot.

Lip: The curling part of the wave as it is falling.

Long-period swell: Open ocean swell with a period of more than 14 seconds. These swells carry their energy deeper, and the wave crests aren't as steep so they are less prone to decay.

Lull: A time between sets of waves, where no waves are breaking.

Macking: Another term for big. Macking waves are big waves.

Mushy: An unfavorable condition, when the waves lack power due to a weak swell, bad tides, or bad wind.

Offshore wind: Offshore winds are usually good for surfing. When the wind is blowing from the shore out to sea, offshore winds groom the face of the wave, holding up the curl line so it falls symmetrically and smoothes out the wave face. Offshore winds are the icing on the cake of a perfect day of surf.

Onshore wind: Onshore winds are usually bad for surfing. When the wind is blowing from the sea and toward shore, they blow over the tops of incoming waves, ruining the symmetry of the curl line and creating bad sections of waves in the wall.

Outside: An expression that surfers yell when a set is approaching. It is also the area from the top of the lineup and out to sea.

Overhead: Some surfers measure waves from the back, some measure from the front and some use the anthropomorphic scale, as in ankle slappers, knee high, head-high, overhead and double and triple overhead, and beyond.

Peak: A wave that breaks both ways, with a right and a left. Or just the top of the wave.

Peeling: A description of what a wave does when it breaks down the line.

Period: Short for **swell period**, which is the amount of time it takes for two consecutive wave crests to pass a stationary point. Surfers forecasting an incoming swell look for wave height and also period, because the longer the period, the more energy the swell carries.

Pit: The impact zone, where waves are breaking.

Pitching out: What a wave does when it hits a shallow area in the ocean bottom. Hollow waves "pitch out" more than mushy waves. It is also possible for a surfer to get "pitched out" with the lip if they don't react fast enough.

Point break: A result of wave refraction, point breaks are usually longer, walled-up waves that break around a point or headland, over sand, rock, coral, or lava. Some of the most famous waves in the world are point breaks: Jeffreys Bay in South Africa; Rincon in Puerto Rico; and Noosa Head on the Sunshine Coast of Queensland, Australia.

Pumping: A favorable condition, similar to **going off**, when the waves are big and consistent and seemingly nonstop.

Punchy: An expression for waves that have power.

Racetrack: An expression, usually applied to Indonesian waves, for a shallow section of the reef, where speed is required to avoid getting creamed by the wave and scraped over the reef.

Racy: An expression for fast waves, as the surfer is often racing the falling lip line.

Reef break: A surf spot breaking on rock, coral, or lava. Jaws on Maui is a prime example of a deep-water reef break.

Reflection: When a wave strikes a hard object and bounces some of its energy off into another direction. The Newport Wedge is a prime example of wave reflection as the size and power of the wave is amplified by energy bouncing off the Corona del Mar Jetty to join the next wave and make an even bigger wave.

Refraction: This is the lovely phenomenon that creates point breaks like Malibu, Rincon, and Noosa Head, Australia. A swell approaching a point or headland will have its top slowed and breaking while the part of the swell in deeper water will continue at the same speed. This creates long waves that break from the top and then evenly along the shallow bottom.

Right: When seen from land, a right is breaking to your left. When paddling into a peak, the right is the wave that is breaking to your right. Some famous rights are Jeffreys Bay, South Africa; Backdoor Pipeline, Hawaii; and Lance's in Indonesia.

Rip: Short for **rip current**, where water that has been swept to shore by an incoming wave looks for a way back out. Rip currents can be useful if you know how to use them, but they can also sweep you out to sea and drown you. The best way out of a rip tide is not to swim against it, but to go along it, find its end, and then swim in.

Runoff: A sometimes hazardous condition where streams, rivers, and storm drains bring rainwater out to sea. When the runoff is tainted with chemicals and sewage, as it often is in populated areas, it is a good idea to not go surfing until the water clears.

Santa Ana wind: A Southern California expression for strong offshore winds that roar from the desert to sea in fall and winter. Santa Anas can create perfect surf conditions, but they also are responsible for the seasonal brushfires that plague Southern California. The term is sometimes used by surfers far from Southern California.

Section: A part of the wave that breaks ahead of the curl line. There can be an inside section, outside section, bowl section, and closeout section.

Set: Waves usually arrive in groups, or sets, of waves.

Shallows: Also known as the **boneyard**, where there isn't much water over the ocean bottom, whether it's reef, sand, coral, or lava. The shallows are usually a good place to avoid.

Shape: The shape of a wave can be described in many ways: lined up, closed out, A-frame, perfect, sloppy, barreling, etc.

Shorepound/shorebreak: Where the ocean meets the land, waves finish off, sometimes breaking all at once in the shorepound or shorebreak.

Short-period swell: Groundswell with a wavelength of under 14 seconds. Because the crests are closer together, they are steeper, which makes short-period swells more prone to decay from winds and currents.

Shoulder: The part of the wave that slopes away from the peak, where the curl is not breaking.

Sideshore: Usually unfavorable winds that are between offshores and onshores, blowing across a surf break at an oblique angle from either side.

Sloppy: An unfavorable condition where the shape and power of waves are effected by wind or tides or currents.

Sneaker set: A set of waves that is bigger than the rest, or comes from an unusual direction. In really big waves, sneaker sets are something to be feared.

Soup: The broken foam of a wave as it crumbles forward.

Spit: When a hollow wave breaks, air and foam are trapped in the tube and sometimes expelled horizontally. Pipeline, Teahupoo, and Jaws are waves renowned for their spit.

Storm surge: A volume of water pushed forward onto land in advance of strong winds from an advancing storm. Storm surges from hurricanes have been responsible for countless deaths over history.

Stormy: A generally unfavorable condition when an approaching storm brings short-period waves and contrary winds. Stormy surf can be fun at times, as storm-pushed waves don't rely on the ocean bottom for shape and can have their own power.

Swell: Energy from a period of strong winds that organizes itself into wave trains as it moves through the ocean. When a swell approaches the coast it is identified by its compass direction—south swell, northwest swell, etc.—and surf forecasters rate the quality of the swell by its height and period.

Swell height: The dimension of a swell measured from wave crest to trough.

Swell period: The dimension of a swell measured in seconds from wave crest to wave crest.

Swell shadow: Islands or other obstruction large and small can block swell from a section of coast. For example, the Santa Barbara area is mostly waveless in the summer because of wave shadowing from the Channel Islands.

Trough: The bottom of the wave, or a groundswell, as opposed to the crest.

Tsunami: A Japanese expression that means "harbor wave": a phenomenon produced by shifts in the earth's crust that displace masses of water. Tsunamis can be incredibly destructive and deadly.

Tube: The hollow interior of a wave formed when the crest of a wave falls forward into the trough. Also known as the **curl**, **barrel**, and a hundred other surfer expressions.

Victory at Sea: A poetic expression for a stormy ocean that is unsurfable.

Wave height: An arguable science, as some surfers measure waves from the back, some from the front, and some by body parts. Wave height is very prone to exaggeration.

Wave train: Energy fanning out from an area of fetch will organize itself by similar wavelengths into wave trains. When these wave trains arrive at a beach, they break as sets of waves.

Wave: When a swell moves out of deep water into shallower water, the energy in the bottom of the swell feels the bottom and topples over, breaking as a wave.

Wedge: A steep, hard-breaking part of a wave, sometimes caused by wave energy reflecting off a hard surface. Sebastian Inlet in Florida, Duranbah in Australia, and the Newport Wedge in California are well-known wedge waves.

Whitecap: Small wavelet caused by local winds blowing over the ocean surface. Surfers look at whitecaps to determine how local winds are blowing and what is the desirable place to surf.

Wind duration: The amount of time wind blows over open water. Wind duration plus wind speed plus the area of water (fetch) is the equation that creates groundswells and then waves.

Windswell: Waves created by winds and local storms within 800 or so nautical miles (1,500 kilometers) of the coast. Windswells have not had time to unwrap and organize themselves into groundswells. They are generally not as powerful as groundswells, but they can be consistent.

Wind waves: Short-period, often weak and sloppy waves created by local winds. Not as desirable as waves created by groundswells, but wind waves can be fun to ride.

Because of that, surfers have a lot of terms to describe wind conditions: blown out, clean, offshore, sideshore, bumpy, choppy, side-onshore, glassy, dead glass, hot and glassy, morning sickness, Victory at Sea, evening glass off.

Offshore winds are generally the icing on the cake that surfers look for. Offshore winds are actually winds blowing from the land toward the waves, so the term is a little confusing. But what offshores do is blow into the wave face, and the effect is like hair gel on a rock star: offshore winds hold up the breaking lip of a wave and generally groom waves into the kinds of shapes and speeds that surfers like best. Offshore winds are like good grooming: they hold back the lip of the wave so it falls in perfect order; and at the same time, smoothes the wave face.

Perfect waves generally aren't perfect without a bit of offshore winds blowing on them. Take a look at photos of perfect waves at Pipeline and Jeffreys Bay and Maverick's and the Mentawai and you will see foam being blown up and back and over the wave, as the curl line falls crisply and perfectly in a symmetry not often seen in nature.

Offshore winds can sometimes be too strong. Malibu has a problem with this in that offshore winds up to about 15 miles per hour (24 kilometers per hour) are ideal and turn a generally slow wave into something world class. But anything stronger than 15 miles per hour (24 kilometers per hour) and offshore winds put a lot of chop and cross-currents into the face of the wave and make the wave a lot harder—and even impossible—to ride. Malibu is not a powerful or fast wave, and sometimes a strong wind blowing at a surfer will be stronger than the wave force moving him forward.

Onshore winds can sometimes help a day of surfing. Big-wave riders in Hawaii sometimes prefer onshore winds because they give a push forward into the wave while offshore winds will get under a surfboard and prevent it from getting into the wave.

But in general, onshore winds are a plague to good surfing conditions. Onshores are winds blowing off the ocean and over the tops of incoming waves. They crumble the curl line and create "sections" in waves that break forward out of sync with the rest of the wave. Onshore winds range from a nuisance to a complete washout of a day of surfing.

The typical pattern in most of California is for a day to start with calm winds or maybe light offshores—**morning sickness** is the expression for an ill wind blowing onshore as the sun is coming up.

As the sun rises and the land heats up, the hot water rises and creates a vacuum that is filled by cooler winds coming off the ocean. Depending on the season a lot of California surf spots are **blown out** by noon, and there is a period of several hours when surfers go home, take a nap or maybe even get some work done, and then return for the **evening glass off** when the onshore winds abate and are replaced by glassy conditions, or offshore winds—as all that wind that has rushed onto land from the sea is pushed back out to sea by cooling air descending back from the upper atmosphere.

Talk the Talk

Jeffreys Bay is a surfspot in the Eastern Cape province of South Africa.

The **Mentawai Islands** are a chain of some 70 islands off the western coast of Sumatra, Indonesia, famed for their surfing.

chapter 7

Surf Etiquette

FIRST POINT MALIBU is quite possibly the most crowded, least polite, most chaotic surf spot in the world. Some say that Australia's Super Bank is worse for surfers taking off in front of each other and competing for waves. But the surfers at Super Bank are experienced—they know what they're doing. The problem with First Point is that it's only 20 minutes from the huddled millions of Southern California, and in this age of surf forecasts that predict swells two weeks in advance and surf cameras that scan the sacred surf zone like a prison yard and effectively beam surfers into the lineup, First Point doesn't have a chance.

Ideally, surfing should be one surfer for one wave. But in this crowded world today, a whole crowd of surfers often try to drop into the same wave. The series of rules known as surf etiquette must be obeyed to prevent injuries and allow everyone to find their wave. *Epic Stock/Shutterstock.* *Inset:* Surfboards await beachside. *Shutterstock*

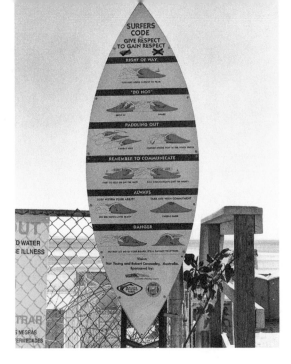

This sign at Malibu was inspired by Australian world champion Nat Young, who was severely beaten up by another surfer at the Australian surf spot Angourie in March 2000. The incident also inspired Young to write a book about crowding and localism and etiquette called *Surf Rage*. *Mari Stanley, courtesy Association of Surfing Lawyers and Nat Young.*

First Point is surfed by devotees who have been riding the waves here for 40 years, and it's attempted by surfers who have been in the ocean for not even 40 minutes. Like oil and vinegar, the crowd at Malibu very often doesn't mix well.

First Point isn't always crowded. There are easy days there when the waves range from poor to so-so to "Why isn't it crowded here?" And on those days Malibu can be fun, the people can be pleasant, and surfing can be what it's supposed to be: a fun way to get some exercise and de-stress.

But those days, sadly, are the exception. For the most part, First Point Malibu is a zoo—a free-fire zoo that brings together longtime locals and clueless visitors in swift collision. And those collisions are visible every couple of minutes and sometimes several times on each wave.

At Malibu you will see the whole wide spectrum of bad behavior in surfing. Everything that surfers shouldn't do to each other, surfers do to each other.

The first commandment of surfing should be: One surfer for one wave. Malibu is a long, easy wave that can handle more than one rider on a wave, but on a good day, if you were to stand at the Wall and count how many surfers take off on each wave, the number would average out to six or seven.

When six or seven surfers take off on the same wave at Malibu, some will fall behind and not make it because they took off too deep or went too slow; they get passed by. At some time on any given wave at Malibu, there will be three or four people all up and riding in the same part of the wave, where there should only be one.

Sometimes the three or four surfers know what they are doing and can stay out of each other's way—sometimes. Other times, one or several of the surfers will do something dumb, or someone paddling out will do something dumb, or someone paddling into the wave will see four surfers all coming at them and they'll still take off—which is dumb—and the result is like NASCAR for the blind: collisions, derision, cuts, bruises, dings, lost boards, swimming, oaths, and recriminations.

Stand at the Wall at Malibu on an average to good day, and that is what you will see, all day long, sunrise to sunset: a total disregard for the long-established rules of surfing. It's painful to watch and even more painful to be a part of.

It's not that the surfers of Malibu don't abide by the rules, it's that they don't seem to know that any rules exist at all.

And it's nothing new. Malibu was one of the first surf spots to become popular as the surfin' sensation swept the nation in the early 1960s. The movie *Gidget* popularized surfing in 1959, and the spot it popularized was Malibu. First Point was one of the first surf spots to become overcrowded as surfing became popular. According to Malibu surfers around then who are still around now, Malibu was even more crowded in the 1960s, and that same volatile mix of experienced surfers and beginners was even more dangerous then, because surfboards were bigger and heavier, and no one wore surf leashes.

The invention of the surf leash in the 1970s made surfing both safer and more dangerous, because now the timid person who was afraid to swim after a surfboard no longer had to, so the waters became even more crowded. Bad surfers who would normally have lost their surfboards were now attached to them, and that dialed up the intensity of the crowds at Malibu even more.

Some say it was the surf leash that brought on the territorial phenomenon known as "localism," which Matt Warshaw defined in *The Encyclopedia of Surfing*: "Territorial practice whereby resident surfers in a given area try to exclude nonresident surfers through threat, intimidation and occasional violence; a predictable, if rarely defensible, surf world response to overcrowding."

Sharks

Many beginner surfers worry about sharks. But veteran surf instructor Carla Rowland says, "Maybe you will see a small sandshark go swimming by, but it's more afraid of you than you are of it. The other surfers are what you should be worrying about, not sharks. Worry about other surfers."

Watching Out for Other Surfers

SAFETY IS ALWAYS a consideration when going into the ocean, as there are dangers lurking below and above. Carla Rowland says, "My number-one goal is to keep my students safe: From the ocean, from the other surfers, from themselves. Surfing is dangerous. People can't drive without a driver's license, so people shouldn't get on a surfboard if they don't know how to ride it. But as much as I try to protect my students, they are still at the whim of the ocean— of Mother Nature— and those forces will do as they please. The moment you think you've got it under control, you get tossed on your cookies. And that can be a traumatic experience, getting tumbled around under water, in the ocean."

Bad surf etiquette. The surfer at right had the right of way—only to have the other surfer flagrantly drop in on his wave and steal the ride away. *Michelle Geft*

Out of the 1960s and into the 1970s and 1980s, most of the surf spots of California and Australia had a local crew who tried to maintain control, often with great vengeance and furious anger. In the 1980s, The Surf Punks were a Malibu-based band who sang about localism in songs like "Somebody Ripped My Stick" and "Locals Only." The band's song "My Beach" summed up the attitude of the territorial local with great eloquence and furious anger:

My beach
My chicks
My waves
Go home!

The ocean is one of the few lawless places left in the world, and through the 1980s and into the twentieth century, acts of violence and vandalism related to surfing became increasingly severe. Courts that had overlooked acts of surfing assault began imposing increasingly serious fines, leading up to a sentence of nine months in jail for an incident in Ventura, California, in the summer of 2000.

The penalties for assault are serious in California, and that is why you will hear a lot of barking at Malibu but see little biting or fighting. Take one punch at someone and you will end up in court for years and jail for months. It's just not worth it, and that is another factor that has made the crowd situation at Malibu so out of control: surf forecasts, plus surf cameras, plus the popularity of surfing, plus the fear of being arrested all adds up to Trouble.

In the first years of the twenty-first century, the Association of Surfing Lawyers attempted to impose some order on the lineup at Malibu. They installed a sign along the sidewalk at the top of the stairs, which lead down to the parking lot, which leads through the wall and past the Pit, and out to the surfline—where trouble is brewing, or fixing to. The sign was inspired by Nat Young, a world champion surfer who suffered a brutal beating by another surfer at the Australian surf spot Angourie in March 2000. That incident inspired Young to write a book about crowding and localism and etiquette called *Surf Rage*, and that book lead to this sign.

A well-intentioned move by the Association of Surfing Lawyers and the Malibu Surfing Association was soon removed by the City of Malibu, as the attorneys had not applied for a permit.

So the sign came down, which was and is a travesty.

A sign stating the rules probably wouldn't have had any effect on the feeding frenzy that erupts at Malibu any time the surf is more than 2 feet (60 centimeters), but the thought was nice.

In fact all of the thoughts expressed on that sign were and are nice, and lay a solid foundation for good etiquette that should be applied to Malibu and everywhere else in the surfing world.

GIVE RESPECT TO GAIN RESPECT

The truth is, beginning surfers are better off finding some lesser-quality surf break where other surfers are few or nonexistent. Learning to surf is difficult enough when a beginner is learning to use new muscles, get used to the surfboard and equipment, deal with their various strengths and fears, and learn the ways of the ocean.

That difficulty is magnified by the proximity of other surfers—whether they be other beginners or more experienced surfers. At many surf spots, it is a common sight to see beginning surfers paddling along like baby ducks, timid in the face of a crowd onslaught, either getting in the way of other surfers and causing accidents, or afraid to get in the way of other surfers and sitting way out of the surf zone, halfway to the pier, where all they will catch will be pneumonia.

Ideally, beginning surfers will learn to paddle and handle the board and catch waves in a place where the waves are less than ideal. But if a beginner is paddling out where there are other surfers it's a good idea to mind manners. Stay away from other surfers. Don't paddle in front of them to catch a wave. Don't get caught paddling in the impact zone when other surfers are riding waves.

It is a too-common occurrence to be riding a wave going directly at a beginning surfer frozen like a deer in the headlights. They don't have control over themselves, their boards, or the situation, and very often they will do the wrong thing, throw their surfboards away, or get in the way of other surfers and cause unrest.

Respect other surfers by staying out of their way, and the best way to do that is find a lesser spot where there are as few surfers as possible. Get your skills down in privacy and isolation, and when you have some idea of what you are doing, move into the more crowded breaks.

RIGHT OF WAY

In any wave situation, one surfer will be paddling into a wave closer to the breaking part of the wave than are the other surfers. That surfer has the **right of way**. This is a fairly easy rule that is broken constantly, at Malibu and everywhere around the world.

The surfer who is closest to the curl has right of way—but that becomes a problem when two surfers of equal ability try to out-paddle each other as a wave is approaching, to position themselves closest to the curl so the other has to get out of the way. You will see this often at surf contests, but also at crowded surf breaks where there is some attempt to maintain decorum. This leads to a lot of paddle battles as surfers try to out-position each other, sitting "deeper" in the lineup, which means closest to the curl.

If everyone in the surfing world honored this simple rule—the surfer closest to the peak has right of way—then all would be well.

But in this crowded world, at any surf spot the human energy usually overwhelms the ocean energy. People get frustrated and bored and desperate, the rules blow away in the wind, and violations are flagrant.

SNAKING OR DROPPING IN: DON'T DO IT

Snaking and dropping in are two sides of the same coin. These are both surfer terms describing the various aggressive ways surfers break surfing's First Law: One surfer per wave.

Talk the Talk

The surfer paddling into a wave closer to the breaking part of the wave than are the other surfers has the **right of way**.

A **paddle battle** is a race between surfers to get into a curl first and thus gain the right of way.

Snaking is the act of paddling under, around, or over the top of another surfer to get position on a wave to be the surfer taking off closest to the curl and earn the right of way. Generally, surfers sit in a lineup based on their knowledge of how the waves are breaking and their own personal knowledge of the best place for them to sit to make the wave. Better surfers tend to sit deeper—or closer to the curl—because they have the ability and the speed to make the wave from farther down the line. Often, ability alone will determine who has position and right of way on a wave, but when the waves are very good or very crowded, that falls apart and surfers will paddle under, around, or over the top of other surfers to get position.

Don't do it. Snaking causes tension and unrest, leads to fights, and generally ruins the good vibration that all surfers seek in the water.

Dropping in is even worse. The act of dropping in means one surfer will be up and riding and into their turn and speed routine, and another surfer will fla-grantly paddle into the wave and ride it in front of the surfer who has the best position and right of way.

Dropping in is a common sight. At places like Malibu, there is generally not a consistent wave, which means the sets of waves are often spaced as much as an hour apart and there are sometimes no more than three or six waves in a set—and sometimes there is just one. Inconsistent swells allow surfers to regroup and bunch up and sit and wait, impatiently, for the next set of waves to come in. When that happens, surfers who have as much as an hour of waiting invested will forget all rules and decorum and just go. The result is that the better surfers taking off deep will get dropped in on by one, two, three, four, or as many as seven surfers at a time. And even at a relatively slow wave like Malibu, that causes a great deal of barking, but little biting. Half the surfers out at Malibu are attorneys, so it's rare to see people actually throwing punches.

But if you want to start a fight, or get tackled, or have someone spear their surfboard into your back, dropping in is a great way to provoke that kind of behavior.

Don't do it.

WHEN PADDLING OUT, PADDLE WIDE

When paddling out to a surf break, it is the responsibility of the paddler to steer clear of other surfers riding waves. The surfer who is up and riding has the right of way, and anyone paddling out has to stay clear of the curl and the surfer in the curl, or near the curl.

The easiest way to prevent collisions is to paddle wide around the lineup when paddling back out to where you will sit to catch the wave. More experienced surfers will paddle closer to the breaking waves in hopes of catching a wave that a surfer has kicked out of or wiped out on. When your skills are better and you know what you are doing and can stay close to the impact zone without causing disasters, then go for it.

Talk the Talk

Snaking is the aggressive act of paddling under, around, or over the top of another surfer to get position on a wave. It's also known as **burning**, **ruining**, **cutting off**, **shoulder-hopping**, or **fading**.

Dropping in is snaking in front of a surfer who is already riding a wave.

A surfer paddles out, staying wide around the lineup and the breaking waves.
Jeanne Hatch/Shutterstock

But as a beginner you are going to want to stay out of the way of other surfers. While that is good for safety and health, it's not always good for catching waves. At Malibu, on slightly bigger days, there are often a lot of smaller waves breaking "inside"—closer to the beach and to the point—that are perfect for beginning surfers. But few beginning surfers have the nerve to sit inside there and catch those waves, because they are intimidated by all the surfers sitting outside, and the waves coming through, and the lines of whitewater they have to deal with when bigger waves break outside of them.

WHEN CAUGHT INSIDE, STAY IN THE WHITEWATER

Sitting inside is a good strategy for when your skills are better and you are more comfortable dealing with whitewater and you have some idea of how waves are breaking and where surfers are going on them.

But for the beginner: Paddle wide to stay out of trouble. Look for the person sitting farthest away from the curl and paddle around them. Do this and you will stay out of the way of more experienced surfers.

Fail to do this and you could end up flailing in the impact zone, getting hit by bigger waves, or getting in the way of other surfers and causing collisions, getting hurt, dinging your surfboard or someone else's surfboard, or losing your board into the rocks.

REMEMBER TO COMMUNICATE

Sometimes other surfers are nice—especially if you are a pretty girl in a bikini—and they will yell "Go!" when you are paddling for a wave in front of them. Sometimes "Go!" also sounds close to "No!" which means "Don't go!" so keep your ears peeled.

Talk the Talk

The **whitewater** or **whitewash** is the foamy, white-colored water created where a wave breaks.

At Malibu there is a lot of yelling and "Hey!ing" and other communication. Some of it is done in angry tones, but some of it is a part of the protocol. If you take off on a wave and there are surfers down the line paddling into the wave, it's a good idea to make some noise to let them know you are coming—as they are focused on catching the wave and are probably barking at the people in front of them.

So say "Hey!" or "Behind you!" or "Get out of the way!" and see if they cooperate. Most surfers will get out of the way when alerted, but there are many others who will look you right in the eye, as a coyote looks at a rabbit, and they'll just go.

Malibu is a wave that breaks mostly to the right, but there are other waves that break in a peak—with a right or left shoulder. In these situations, sometimes surfers will "split a peak"—one going right, one going left—and in that circumstance, surfers will communicate their intentions: "Going right!" "Going left!" When this cooperation happens, it's nice. But when tensions are high in a lineup, communication goes down to zero and that is when accidents happen.

ALWAYS SURF WITHIN YOUR ABILITY

Just as a beginning surfer will walk into a surf shop and buy the hottest thing on the rack, even when that surfboard is completely inappropriate, so too will beginning surfers attempt to surf those beautiful waves they have seen in magazines and videos—from Malibu to Pipeline, Ningaloo Reef in Australia to Guethary, France.

But where buying an expensive, inappropriate board is a hazard to your finances (and your ego), attempting to surf a wave that is beyond your ability can be hazardous to your health—and the health of those around you.

Again, this is a big problem at Malibu, because First Point especially is a wave that is easily accessible to a population of millions of people, and it's a wave that is easy to approach, even on the bigger days.

Because Malibu is a point break, and because it tends to be inconsistent, with long lulls even on the biggest days, Malibu is inviting to beginning surfers who walk to the top of the point and paddle out in the gap between First Point and Second Point or who paddle off the beach. That mixture of rank beginners with intermediate surfers and experienced surfers is what makes Malibu so frustrating and dangerous.

Malibu is a great beginners spot, except that it's too crowded. In the Malibu area there are other spots that are better for beginners: Sunset is an average break at the end of Sunset Boulevard that is not a good enough wave to attract more experienced surfers, but is just right for beginners: long and slow and crowded by other beginners.

Just up the beach from Malibu, the inside part of Third Point is a cove where whitewater and small waves break into a small cove. The bottom is rocky, but it's still perfect for beginners, as the more experienced surfers stay outside and there is no intermingling of the classes.

Zuma Beach is another place that is good for beginners, because it is a wide, flat, long beach with plenty of room for everyone. That is where beginners should go to seek and find the perfect beginner wave on the perfect beginner day and be alone with their thoughts.

ALWAYS PADDLE HARD

In a crowded situation, every move you make is going to be watched like a wolf watching its prey: If you are hesitant or weak or paddle for a wave and pull back, you will quickly be ignored, and the whole world will drop in on you.

Catching waves requires commitment, and that applies to experienced surfers riding giant days and beginners just learning to catch waves and stand.

Paddle hard. Commit yourself. Timidity doesn't cut it in the ocean.

DO NOT LET GO OF YOUR BOARD:
IT'S A DANGER TO OTHERS

One of the complaints that surfers in the 1970s had about surf leashes was that surfers used them as a crutch, in place of using experience and skill. Before leashes, surfers had to worry about wipeouts, because a wipeout usually meant a lost board, and a long swim, and the possibility of damaging, breaking, or losing your surfboard. Surfers had to hold onto their board in a death grip when they were caught inside a breaking wave.

But the leash as a crutch also applied to situations where surfers were confronted by breaking waves, or other surfers, and the leash allowed them to let their boards go lose so they could save their own skins while putting others at risk.

You will see this at any crowded surf spot all too often: Inexperienced surfers get into panic situations and they let go of their boards and dive for the bottom.

This is a bad idea for yourself and those around you, and a habit you should not get into in the beginning. If you are caught inside a breaking wave, take the pain. Take the wave on your head and do your best to hold onto your board. That can mean duck diving under it, or turning turtle or holding onto the nose of your board and swimming through.

It is easier to let go of your board and dive under the wave and avoid taking a beating, but you are endangering anyone behind or around you, and also yourself, because that loose board could come back and clobber you—or your leash could break and you will have to swim.

Hold onto your board. Good habits are good.

chapter 8

Mastering the Waves

CROWDS, ONSHORE WINDS, stingrays, sunburn, wetsuit rashes, rip-currents, fear of drowning, fear of stepping on a sea cucumber, fear of embarrassment—there are myriad barriers and obstacles to overcome when learning to surf. Some of the obstacles are physical, some mental. But one of the biggest barriers to learning to surf is eternal: Time.

Left: Mastering the waves is all a question of time and tide—lots of time to practice and the cooperation of the ocean's tides. *Shutterstock. Right:* Surfing soon becomes not just a sport, but an obsession—and a magnificent one, too. *Fernando Jose Vasconcelos Soares/Shutterstock*

It takes time to learn how to surf. A surf instructor might guarantee "Stand Up On Your First Wave!" and that often will come true. But once the instructor goes away and you are left alone to face the mysteries of the sea—and your own strengths and weaknesses—the learning curve from complete landlubber to the beginning of competency as a surfer takes time.

Heaps of time, mate.

ONE OF THE KEYS TO LEARNING TO SURF IS STAYING WITH IT
The ocean is not always cooperative, and waiting for ideal conditions takes time. Tide, wind, swell, sandbars, and other natural factors have to settle down long enough to make conditions that are best for learning to surf: easy, rolling waves, not much wind.

Those conditions change from hour to hour, morning to afternoon, day to day, and season to season. Even if a person has absolutely nothing else to do and lives somewhere like Hawaii, where the water is warm, tides are minimal, and the ocean is active, there are only so many hours you can surf in a day.

Learning to surf is easier when you are young, because time stretches out; the summer that is over in a flash to a teenager or an adult seems to last a lifetime for young surfers. Learning to surf requires hours and hours and hours of ocean time: seeing the ocean in all its moods, to know all its moods; paddling for miles and miles to develop back and shoulder and arm muscles; learning how to line up a wave, how to catch a wave, how to stand up on a wave, how to angle on a wave.

Staying With It

The key to learning to surf is to stay with it. Surfing is indeed an obsession—if you're going to get good at it, that is.

So the key to learning to surf is: Stay with it.

Some surfers will jump up on a soapbox and thump their chests and declare that "Surfing isn't a sport, it's a way of life. An obsession!" And in a way, they are right, especially at the beginning, because surfing requires a certain obsessiveness and a willingness to overcome many obstacles by land and sea.

Learning to surf isn't easy, at first. It's cold, scary, frustrating, embarrassing. Even if you are riding a Softop over soft sand in soft surf, you are still going to come out with cuts and bruises, soreness in muscles you never knew you had. The ocean can be ominous, waves are daunting, those unseen squishy and stinging critters under the sea are frightening, and those surfers on the surface, all cursing and battling and pushing each other off waves, are even scarier than the critters.

But stay with it.

Put in the time.

Pay your dues.

The ocean is going to punish you like a sorority/fraternity humiliation: slap you around, try to drown you. But that is all part of the initiation. Some beginners will try it once, find that it's a lot harder than it looks, quit, and go snowboarding.

But those who hang in there will be rewarded in ways obvious and not so obvious: sunrises and sunsets, dolphins swimming under your board, nature putting on the Greatest Show on Earth.

But the best thing about it is learning a mastery of those waves that were at first so intimidating: "I'll never be able to ride those waves! I'll never be able to do that!"

Stick with it, and you will.

But none of it is easy, and it all takes time.

TOTAL INVOLVEMENT: LONGBOARDS, SHORTBOARDS, OR BOTH

Here in the twenty-first century, there is a remarkably wide variety of surfboard shapes, sizes, designs, and materials. Beginning surfers don't really need to worry about all the possibilities and variations of longboard, shortboard, Fish, Thruster, twin-fin, epoxy, balsa, carbon fiber, popout, custom-shaped, Softop, etc. But as you progress as a surfer, that whole world of options is going to open up to you, and one of the first forks in the road you will face will be this: longboard or shortboard?

Pro surfer Keegan Edwards shows pure shortboard form—but while riding on a longboard. There was a time when high-performance Total Involvement surfing was at odds with traditional longboard surfing. But as the two kinds of riding blended over the last few decades, and technology provided boards that were lighter and better, longboard surfers began riding their boards like shortboards. Here, Edwards competes in China's Annual Longboard contest at Waikiki in 2009. *Mana Photo/Shutterstock*

Modern surfboards cut across waves like precision surgical instruments. This surfer rides to the top of the wave, then does a big snap off the crest to get speed for what waits down the line. *Epic Stock/Shutterstock*

For many surfers, the longboard will never go out of fashion. *Lucia Griggi*

Surfboard Diversity Training

Learn to surf on a longboard, then try riding all other
types of surfboard—it's one of the joys of surfing, as each
one offers a different experience.

The big divide between longboards and shortboards goes back to the 1967 World Contest at Ocean Beach, San Diego, where Australian surfer Nat Young on a cut down board called Sam surfed with what he called "Total Involvement"—surfing on the tail and turning in and around the curl, doing cutbacks, turning off the lip. At the same time, Hawaiian David Nuuhiwa was riding a more traditional longboard, putting his feet on the nose as much as possible to ride in the traditional "noseriding" style.

Nat Young won the World Contest, and that drew a dividing line between longboards and shortboards that has been snaking and pulsing ever since. Through most of the twentieth century, longboarders thought shortboarders were arrogant punks with no style. Shortboarders thought longboarders were children of a lesser god, forced to hack around on big lumber because of various physical or spiritual or stylistic flaws. The two just couldn't get along.

Then, in the 1990s, surfers like Jay Moriarity and Joel Tudor rode longboards in a way that began to chip away the dust. Longboarding became cool again.

Now, in the twenty-first century, most surfers will begin on longboards and at some point progress to shorter boards. Ultimately, they will be faced with this fork in the road: Should they go long or short?

The answer to that is ride both. Ride them all.

One of the modern joys of surfing is the incredible diversity of surfboards that are out there, everything from nouveau retro *alaia* to carbon-fiber longboards, and a hundred varieties in between. Stand-ups, Fish, stubbs, and more.

Learn to surf on a longboard, then progress to a shortboard—and then ride them all.

PADDLING OUT IS AS MUCH BRAIN AS IT IS BRAWN

Ocean Beach, San Francisco, is the wild, ragged edge of a great California city. All is not quiet on that western front, because the elements come together in swift collision along the 4 miles (6 kilometers) of sandy beach between the Golden Gate and Fleishacker's Pool.

The Golden Gate is one of the factors that makes Ocean Beach arguably the hardest place to surf in the world. It's not that the waves are more or less difficult, although Ocean Beach when it's really bombing and the offshores are pouring down from Sutro Tower is a triple black diamond situation: Big, beautiful A-frame peaks that are devilishly hard to catch.

What makes Ocean Beach so hard is just getting out there. With all of that tidal movement in and out of the Golden Gate, plus the North Pacific gobbing endless lines of swell from Russia with love, the 200 yards (180 meters) of impact zone between the beach and outside is like a reverse of the D-Day invasion. To get a wave on a big day at Ocean Beach, or even a medium-sized day, a surfer has to get through that 100-yard (90-meter) kill zone of exploding waves, tricky currents, and seemingly endless, impenetrable lines of whitewater—all of it pushing toward the beach with infinitely more force than any human can muster.

Paddling Skills

Paddling out requires muscle, strong paddling, and knowing how to push through waves, turn turtle, and duck dive—as well as ocean skills, such as recognizing currents, spotting holes in the reef or sandbar, timing sets.

To make it **out the back** on a big day at Ocean Beach takes as much brains as it does brawn. The surfers who have it figured out will take an overview from the sand dunes for a long time, watching other surfers paddle for an hour only to get beat back to the beach, while looking at the kill zone for holes and channels and currents and cross currents. Paddling out at Ocean Beach takes strategy: starting at this point and hooking into that rip current and timing the sets to have a chance to make it out within the lulls—if there are any lulls.

Ocean Beach is Extreme Paddling. In many ways, it's the ultimate test of a surfer's strength and wit for making it through the impact zone and out to sea to snag one of those big, beautiful offshore peaks that are so close, and yet so far away.

Paddling out becomes important as a beginning surfer progresses to an intermediate stage and starts to surf waves with a higher degree of difficulty. Most beginner breaks, like Malibu and Waikiki and Cowell's Beach, are beginner breaks in part because they are easy places to paddle out: wide flat beaches with lots of area outside the impact zone where beginning surfers can paddle tentatively out, then work their way to where the waves are breaking.

Paddling out requires muscle and paddling skills as well as knowing how to push through and turn turtle and duck dive and get under breaking waves and lines of whitewater. But paddling out also requires ocean skills, similar to what the Ocean Beach guys learn: recognizing channels and currents and holes in the reef or sandbar, timing sets to know when to start paddling, devising clever ways to get around and under breaking waves and out the back.

This all comes with practice and experience and taking a lot of lumps. As surfers progress from beginner to intermediate, they are going to turn turtle and get the board ripped from their hands. They are going to try to push through waves and go over the falls. Caught inside, pushed around, half drowned. It's all part of the learning curve, and at the very top of the curve are places like Ocean Beach—the ultimate test of a basic act: getting out the back.

THE DUCK DIVE: FORM FOLLOWS FETISH

Duck diving is an advanced technique, but something to look forward to. It's not just a clever way to dodge a breaking wave and not get detonated; it's also pleasing to the eye and it feels good, as you are bending yourself and your board into the power pockets of the wave and using that energy to get yourself under and out the back, as the wave explodes behind you. Duck diving is somewhere between a toreador fighting a bull and an underwater ballet. Getting under danger gracefully is what duck diving is all about.

Looks good, feels good.

Duck diving is the expert, black-diamond technique for getting under waves that begins with simply pushing through. The beginning ways of getting under and through waves are pushing through or turning turtle. You can push through paddling prone or kneeling, and if you really

Out the back means paddling through the breaking waves and "out the back" into the smoother ocean to turn around to catch waves going in.

Duck diving is an art—both in its performance and the beauty of its form. This surfer bends himself and his board into the pocket of the wave over a reef in the Maldives, then uses that energy to dive under and out the back. *Lucia Griggi*

want to show off, you can stand up on your board as you roll through a wave or let a wave roll under or around you.

Bailing out is a method you want to avoid, but sometimes it's unavoidable. When confronted by a hard-breaking wave in the impact zone, a wall of rolling whitewater, or a wave so big it terrifies you right down to your DNA, sometimes the only thing is to throw away your board, leaving it to the whims of Creation—and swim for the bottom. Bailing out is a bad habit to get into, because flung boards can bean other surfers.

Duck diving is a great technique for getting under or through trouble. When paddling toward a wave that is breaking, and it's too big to push through or turn turtle, and bailing out is not an option due to personal credo or a lot of big

Duck Diving

Duck diving is all about getting *under* danger gracefully.

Duck Diving Tips From a Pro

GARRETT MCNAMARA'S
LIFE OR DEATH DUCK DIVE

Garrett McNamara is a Hawaiian resident who has been surfing nonstop since the 1970s. He has ridden the world's best waves and the world's biggest waves and he has been caught inside all of them, from Haleiwa to Pipeline, Jaws to Maverick's—and even collapsing glaciers in Alaska.

Garret has has also taken some of the world's biggest waves on his head. He has a great deal of experience getting out of heaps of trouble or caught on the wrong side of the peak in the middle of a ship-killing ocean. He was kind enough to share his experience in situations the rest of us will probably never be in—or hope we won't.

"I started just like everyone else, wrapping my legs around the board when I got caught inside, or turning turtle. Duck diving is a technique that began in Hawaii, I think, because it's a cool thing to do when the water is clear, and it will also keep you from getting pounded and sent to the beach with a broken board.

"Also, at some places in Hawaii, like Pipeline, sometimes you don't wear leashes, and so duck diving is crucial for staying out and getting more waves.

"Pipeline is duckable totally, as long as you are using a small enough board. At Pipeline sometimes I'll be confronted with big lines of whitewater and it's kind of a tossup whether to bail or duck dive. If you bail it's an easy, mild pounding and then you have to fish for your board. If you

duck dive and do it wrong you are going to get shook up really bad and won't be able to paddle back out fast.

"But if you watch the guys who are good at Pipeline—Andy Irons and Kelly Slater and Bruce Irons and Jamie O'Brien—they'll go right at Pipeline and kick out and paddle straight back out, no matter what is coming—whitewater or a bomb set, and they almost always power through and make it. But those are the best surfers in the world, and their paddling and duck diving ability is part of that.

"But sometimes you get lucky at Pipeline. Even when the wave explodes right in front of you, you can get under it somehow, in the hole carved out by the explosion, and it pops you right out the back.

"A lot of that is luck, and some of it is skill—knowing you are in the right spot. I would say it's seventy-five percent luck and twenty-five percent skill—maybe even eighty percent and twenty percent.

"You can duck dive big Teahupoo, but not giant Teahupoo—but you have to do it just right. Giant Teahupoo you have no chance. Every bit of water is being lifted up off the reef, and it will just take you over with it. But if you are caught inside on a giant day at Teahupoo, you have all kinds of problems.

"Big waves over forty feet [12 meters] are usually impossible to duck dive, but some guys pull it off. Of all the situations I have been in, the most scared I have ever been was at Jaws, in a situation where I had to duck through a huge wave, and I don't want to think about what would have happened if I had done it wrong.

mean guys paddling behind you, then the only option is to press the rails and kick the tail.

Duck diving done right is form and function coming together in a way that will save your hide. And it is done in two phases. Speed, positioning, and timing are crucial in the proper implementation of a successful duck dive. The object of the exercise is to use the energy and flow of an oncoming wave, push the nose of the board down to get under the wave and then push down on the tail with your knee or your foot—or both.

Done right, the initial pushing down on the nose combined with the upward rush of water pushes you deeper under the wave. It feels cool

"This was a big day at Piahe, on Maui, or Jaws as some people call it. There were some sixty- to seventy-foot [18- to 21-meter] sets, and I was there to tow with my partner Ikaika Kalama. I don't remember the year, but I remember that day Shane Dorian rode a giant left that almost won the XXL Award for Biggest Wave.

"The waves were firing this day, but nothing was right for me. I had the wrong straps on my tow board, and the wind was wrong. It was blowing sideways so some barrels were folding shut, and there were big sections—which are dangerous on a giant day, when wiping out is not an option. You really have to make every wave, because every wipeout could be deadly.

"Tow surfing is a partnership. Your driver has the PWC in his hands, and also your life, because he is putting you into the wave, and on a big day that decision can be life or death. As we drove out there and I told Ikaika: 'Don't put me in deep, put me in a good spot so I can find my own way.'

"But he put me in deep and I rode it as far as I could, but I had to kick out the back because I was behind a section I wasn't going to make. So I kicked out, wearing two life jackets, on a tiny little tow board that was maybe sixteen inches [41 centimeters] wide and an inch [2½ centimeters] thick. Couldn't paddle it really, and couldn't really submerge because those life jackets turned me into a human cork.

"So I kicked out and what do I see but an even bigger wave coming at me, and I am in the zone. Ikaika thought I was still riding and didn't see me kick out early because of the wind—but even if he had known I was in deep trouble, he wouldn't have been able to get me.

"I was in deep trouble, and I knew it, and I also knew my son was on the cliff watching. I also knew the same thing had happened to Brazilian surfer Carlos Burle at Jaws: He got caught inside, he went over the falls and he broke his back and nearly died.

"I barely paddled over the first wave and made it, but the next was even bigger. I was horrified. Really scared because I had been in a lot of situations but I really didn't know if I was going to make it out of this one. The wave was just huge and it was going to get me. I paddled as much as I could and then as the wave started to barrel over me, I jumped off the board and started swimming. I could feel the wave pulling up as I was going down and I thought for sure I was going over the falls. But I kept stroking and I got lucky and somehow popped out the back.

"Ikaika came and got me but that was it for that day. I didn't surf at all that day, and this was a huge day, the kind of day we all wait for.

"I threw in the towel. Put my tail between my legs. Whatever you want to call it. That was the first time I had ever done that.

"The moral to this story is: When you are driving, listen to your partner. And when you are caught in a really bad situation, don't panic. Miracles happen—giant waves can be duck dived, even on a toothpick, wearing two life jackets—but you have to keep a calm head to let that happen."

down there, mixing with all that long-traveled ocean energy, and the beauty of duck diving is knowing that energy and feeling that energy and using it to get away from it.

Timing is everything, especially when starting the duck dive. Knowing when and how hard to push the nose under is crucial. Getting a feel for the wave and knowing when to sink the tail to go a little deeper and then point the nose toward the surface is also part of the maneuver.

Duck diving can be done on a longboard, but it's not easy. The longer and wider the board, the more surface area and flotation there is to sink, hold down, and then push.

Duck diving is part toreador fighting a bull, part underwater ballet. And it's essential to progressing as a surfer to catch ever-larger waves. *Jarvis Gray/Shutterstock*

Most waves can be duck dived, but there are exceptions. Teahupoo at size would be almost impossible to duck dive, because that wave draws every molecule of water off the reef and throws it back on the reef.

Giant waves like Maverick's and Cortes Bank are also difficult to duck dive, because there is so much water moving up and over, not even the strongest surfer can exert enough pressure and power to force a board down, up, and through that energy.

Done right, duck diving looks good, feels good, and will save your hide.

Done wrong, you are going over the falls, maybe taking out paddlers inside of you, breaking your leash, losing your board, swimming through miles of shark-infested waters, over coral reefs, and up onto jagged rocks.

So do it right.

LINING UP AND TRIANGULATION

"Lining up" means using landmarks at sea. This is crucial at any surf spot, but it's especially important at a big wave like Maverick's. The penalty for sitting in the wrong spot at Maverick's when a big set comes is getting **caught inside**. And that is a kind of punishment that is beyond the knowing of most mortals—and even most surfers.

Lining up is the key to catching more waves and avoiding wipeouts. It's something a surfer learns through the natural necessity of wanting to catch more waves. Once beginners are past the initial struggles, they will begin to notice the patterns and movements of the ocean. At some point, beginning surfers will notice that waves tend to break in the same place, and that place can be marked using landmarks and seamarks.

Lining up is a technique that requires you know how the waves are moving, how the currents are moving, and what the tide is doing. You need to know the waves and know yourself in relation to the waves.

Using Malibu as an example, on a typical day at First Point there are waves breaking "outside" along the top of the point, as swell lines come down from Second Point. Some surfers line up out there based on what the wave is doing. Sometimes the swell is angled west up the point and sometimes the swell pushes down the point and the takeoff spot is closer to the pier.

Experienced Malibu surfers know the lineup by look and feel. Others will look inland and use a variety of trees, fences, mountain ridges, and other fixed objects to find their lineup. The two most common objects are the flagpoles at the Adamson House and a stand of palm trees. Surfers sitting up at the top of the point will note which side of the flagpoles the palm trees are on. When they catch the first wave, they calculate if they were in the right takeoff spot or not and adjust their position the next time using the flagpole and the palm trees.

Lineups change as the swell changes intensity, the tide changes, the wind comes up, and with the ebb and pulse of the crowd.

Most beginners will not be sophisticated enough or in control enough to worry too much about lineups, as most beginners will be lining up away from the crowd and away from the peak and at the beginning will be taking whatever scraps of wave energy and foam come their way.

But as skills progress and a beginner inches into the lineup, the necessity to catch more waves will become the mother of more advanced skills. Lining up is one of them, whether you are snagging inside waves at Snapper Rocks off Australia's Gold Coast or dodging sneaker sets at Maverick's.

Talk the Talk

When a surfer is out of position and on the wrong side of a breaking wave, they're **caught inside**. Sometimes to escape, a surfer will try to paddle over, under, or through a breaking wave. Sometimes this works. Other times, it means a big spill.

TURN, TURN, TURN

For the first half of the twentieth century, most surfers went mostly straight. Surfboards were big and heavy, the fin wasn't invented until the late 1930s and so going straight was the style, and it looked good. In the late 1930s, Hawaiian surfers began experimenting with Hot Curl boards that had narrow tails but no fins. These boards could be turned, and rudimentary "hot dog" surfing began along the surf spots of Waikiki. Around 1938 a transplanted Wisconsin/California surfer named Tom Blake attached an aluminum rudder from a boat to a surfboard, and all of a sudden the problem of **sliding ass**—sliding sideways across a wave—was eliminated.

Surfboards became shorter and lighter through the 1940s, as surfers began using lighter balsa wood to make surfboards, and then foam and fiberglass and other plastics to make surfboards easier to carry, easier to paddle, and more maneuverable. Surfing footage of Malibu shot in 1947 shows surfers like Matt Kivlin and Buzzy Trent mostly going straight on big, hardwood surfboards weighing as much as 100 pounds (45 kilograms).

A few years later, in the early 1950s, these surfers are riding Malibu Chips, made of balsa, and they are bottom turning, trimming, cutting back, and looking thoroughly modern.

In the almost 60 years from the early 1950s to now, surfing has had a number of performance revolutions large and small, but one of the larger turning points, so to speak, in the evolution of performance surfing was the 1967 World Contest in Ocean Beach, near San Diego. At that contest, Australian Nat Young rode a shorter board nicknamed Sam and displayed his newfangled **Total Involvement** style of surfing where he surfed from the tail to move his board around the energy pockets in the curl. The Australian defeated David Nuuhiwa, who was surfing from the nose in the more traditional longboard, nose-riding style. Young's Total Involvement won the day—and changed the course of surfing forever.

Since 1967, surfers around the world—in competition or free surfing, screwing off or trying to change the world, accidentally or on purpose—have evolved a complicated repertoire of turns and turn backs, all of them on the cusp of making the wave.

When surfing a point, reef, beachbreak, or any kind of wave that requires anything other than a straight line, turning, for lack of a better word, is good. Whether you are going right or left, turning works. Turning sets up the wave, gets you around, through and over sections, and allows a surfer to stay with the power of the wave, play with the power of the wave, and make it look good and feel good. Turning, in all of its forms; turning for speed, for style, for power, turning has marked the upward evolution of performance surfing. And turning will become important to a surfer passing from beginner to intermediate, and not only will turning help you make more waves and avoid wipeouts, it will open up a whole world of performance surfing.

At some point, a beginning surfer will stop going straight into the beach, and will feel the need for speed, for maneuvers, for doing all the minor and major directions and corrections to angle on a wave, and ride it from the peak to the channel, in one graceful repertoire of bottom turns, top turns, cutbacks, floaters, and an ever-evolving bag of tricks of tail slides, aerials, 360s, and other modern shenanigans.

Turning a surfboard is somewhere on the cusp of form and function. Turning is essential to making a wave, but it's also important to making a surfer—and a wave—look good.

This is an introduction to the various kinds of turns, from the start of the wave, to the end.

Talk the Talk

Sliding ass was old school surfing slang for sliding sideways on waves, which was due in large part to the old school surfboards that lacked fins.

Misaligned

**NAT YOUNG LEARNS THE HARD WAY
TO DOUBLE CHECK HIS LINEUPS**

In 2009, Surfer *magazine ordained Nat Young as the tenth
most important surfer of all-time. An Australian who won
the World Contest at Ocean Beach, San Diego in 1967,
Young was the figurehead of the "total involvement" school
of surfing that ushered in the shortboard era and changed
surfing forever.*

*Young is a surfing legend, but even surfing legends
make mistakes and pay for them. Young told this surf story
to the author about lining up wrong at Waimea Bay.*

"I was staying with Gerry Lopez at the Pipeline House.
This was in the winter of 1983, I think. One morning I got up
before dawn and pedaled up to Sunset, but the swell was too
big up there, so I pedaled back down to Waimea. Waimea was
looking absolutely fantastic. Big clean shadows were stretching across the bay in the first rays of light. It was impossible to
tell how big it was. Just perfect, peeling tubes from one end
of the Bay to the other, and not a soul in the water. I sat there
for twenty minutes just looking at it and thinking, 'This is just
ridiculous. Why isn't somebody riding this bloody thing?'

"Then I thought, 'Well I'm going to do something about it.'

"I pedaled back to Gerry's house thinking I didn't really
have a board for Waimea. Fortunately, Gerry had a full
quiver of boards under his house. I found something that
looked like it would support my volume. I really had no idea
who it belonged to but figured it was okay. When I got back
to the bay, the morning light revealed it was fifteen feet [4½
meters], offshore and perfect. I hadn't surfed it for years.

"I have never really felt confident at the Bay, probably
because when you're in the top bracket of surfers, as I was in
the late 1960s and early 1970s, there's a lot of peer pressure
to ride waves that you would avoid under normal situations.
I'd never surfed Waimea like it looked that morning—empty
and perfect and just so inviting. I'd always surfed it with fear
with loads of other surfers as reference. This time it was different. I was on vacation, it was the best wave I could find at
that time, and it seemed like a good idea.

"I was the first one out. I caught one wave on the edge
and made the drop and that all felt fine. The board felt very
comfortable and I thought, 'Well OK, it's time to set it up off
the old lineup.' The old lineup used to be the church tower
and the last palm tree on the end of the point looking back
toward Log Cabins. Where those two intersected used to

be the perfect takeoff. By the time I'd sorted out the lineup,
there were a couple other people out, but they were sitting
in the channel—or so I thought. It didn't cross my mind
that they might actually be in the right takeoff zone, and I
might be in the wrong spot. I was just working on what had
been a fact. I thought, 'This is fine here. I'll set it all up as I
used to and hopefully get a couple of classic barrels at big,
glassy Waimea.'

"This set came, and it was a big, nasty mother of a set. I
took off on the first wave, dropped straight to the bottom and
ground off a big, heavy bottom turn. About halfway through
the tune, I saw the left starting to peel back straight at me. I
thought, 'What have I done?' I figured I'd better do something,
but I was a rat in a trap. Everything sort of slowed down. It
was a horrendous wipeout, probably the most spacey situation I've ever been in, because the wave broke with so much
power on that ledge. I remember being propelled through
space and my leg rope popping like a piece of string.

"I came up after a long, long time and found myself
along the point and thought, 'My God, what am I doing
here?' I swam out a little bit and got washed around, and I
could see all this blood. My whole face was red and hurting
bad. I made it back to the beach and walked up to the
houses on the point there, dragging Lopez' board behind
me and thinking, 'Jesus, what happened?' Because I didn't
have a clue what I'd done wrong.

"Up on the beach, Lopez was there with Sato, who was
taking pictures. I walked up and said, 'What happened?
What hit me? Where was I? I did everything right. I took the
last palm tree on the end of the point and lined it up with
the bloody church tower. I did everything according to the
book and I got nailed by this huge, bloody left.'

"Everybody started cracking up, and Lopez said, 'You
know, you haven't been here for a few years. Hurricane
Iwa changed a few things.' It turned out the hurricane had
wiped out all the palm trees on the point, and new ones
have been replanted in different places. Lopez said, 'Your
reference point disappeared after that cyclone.' It really
made me feel like I was from another generation, because I
got the shit beat out of me for using old reference points.

"I ended up with about ten stitches in my face. We had
a few beers and laughed about it a few hours later, but I
was pretty disillusioned. I actually haven't surfed Waimea
since then."

A surfer in perfect trim, gathers and maintains all the speed he can from this beachbreak wave and waits to see what the wave will do next, and what he will do with that speed: pull into the tube, do a down the line turn, float over a section, or carve a cutback. *Alain Cassiede/Shutterstock*

Bottom Turn

The first turn on a wave after dropping in. The bottom turn doesn't necessarily always happen at the bottom of the wave. Some waves demand that a surfer angle down the line from take-off, and *go, go, go!* to make it through the initial drop and then the coming sections. There are waves like Maalaea at Maui and Teahupoo in Tahiti where bottom turning is impossible. But on most waves, the sequence is:

1. Paddle.
2. Stand.
3. Drop in, examining the wave as you are dropping in.
4. Timing your bottom turn to set up the wave and what you intend to do next: pull into the barrel, turn off the top, go fast and straight down the line.

There are varieties of bottom turns as well. Some big-wave surfers will **fade** into a wave, carving toward the curl as they drop in, then hitting their bottom turn at just the right time.

But most bottom turns are a variation on drop in, get to the bottom either vertically or diagonally, and use the descent speed to project onto whatever part of the wave is offering itself.

There are several ways to get around a "section" of a wave. This backside surfer could have tucked under the lip of the wave for a tuberide, pulled a floater to go over the section, and come down with the lip—or do what he is doing: carve a bottom turn around the section and maintain his speed to keep going. *Alain Cassiede/Shutterstock*

Nicely slotted in a clean little barrel, this surfer is stalling with his hand in the wave face and his foot on the tail to prolong the good feeling of riding inside the tube. *Alain Cassiede/Shutterstock*

Vertical Turn

Some surfers live to drop in on a wave, turn hard off the bottom, and go straight up to hit the lip of the wave vertically. This is form and function—and also fun, because these turns demand skill, are exciting to do, and generate a lot of speed for whatever is coming next. These vertical turns have a number of names, some of them antiquated, some of them new: **roller coaster**, **off the top**, **off the lip**, **vertical hit**, **lip bash**, **slash**, **carve**, and more.

Again, a surfer turning hard off the top of the wave will change the angle of attack on the turn, depending on what the wave is doing behind, and in front.

Some surfers will use that top turn to drive laterally down the wave, going back up to the top to get some energy to project down the line—particularly on very fast waves.

If a wave is a little forgiving, or if a surfer is very good, sometimes a vertical turn off the top will bring a surfer back down to the trough almost vertically. And if the surfer has skill, there is no speed loss and he will flow into another bottom turn to set up the next turn.

Pro surfer Rob Kelly is a "small-wave wizard," a surfer who can somehow find speed and energy from waves that don't have any speed or energy and then turn that speed into big moves on tiny sections. Here he competes at the 47th East Coast Surfing Championship in Virginia Beach, Virginia, in 2009. *Kimberly Ann Reinick/Shutterstock*

Left: A competitor at the Sri Lankan Pro throws spray doing a snap on a nice lefthander. *Lucia Griggi*

Below: The daughter of a long surfing dynasty, Coco Ho was seen surfing in the movie *Blue Crush*—that was her as a young grommette on the TV. She is now representing Hawaii as a top competitor on the ASP World Tour. This is Coco throwing out her hip and letting her backbone slip, somewhere in the Hawaiian Islands. *Mana Photo/ Shutterstock*

Pumping

Watch Kelly Slater surf Backdoor Pipeline and on many waves he will drop in and not go to the bottom, but turn midway down the face, set his edge, and then do climbing and dropping turns to generate lateral speed down the line. Kelly is an absolute master of this, and uses his size and his physicality to generate great speed and prepare himself for whatever the wave is going to do next.

What used to be called **climbing and dropping** is now called **pumping** or **driving down the line** or other terms. This sort of lateral surfing is done for speed and to make it across the face of a fast wave, or a wave that has sections.

Sometime before resting on the Seventh Day, God created the perfect body for surfing and gave it to Kelly Slater: 5 feet 9 inches (1.75 meters) and 165 pounds (75 kilograms) of flexibility, balance, grace, and speed. Here he is cutting back during round 4 of the Quiksilver Pro on September 27, 2009, in Hossegor, France. *Kirstin Scholtz/ASP/CI via Getty Images*

Some surfers grow up riding small waves and have trouble adjusting to size and power. Coming from the North Shore of Kauai, Andy Irons is the opposite. He's more comfortable in heaving barrels than slop. Andy has had to master waves outside of Hawaii to win world titles. This is Andy doing a "dump floater" on the end section of a small wave during a competition. The more points, the merrier. Here, he rides a wave in the Rip Curl Pro at Bells Beach, Australia, in 2007. *Susan Harris/Shutterstock*

Floater

There was a time when surfers had to go through sections or down around sections to get past crumbling pieces of whitewater. The shortest distance between two points is a straight line, so sometimes straight through a section is the way to go. But if a section isn't hollow, or if it's crumbling or if it's too long for a surfer to go through, the surfer would have to go around, bottom turning again around the section and hoping to have enough speed to get to the other side. Beginning in the 1980s, surfers began **floating** over sections, using their speed to fly over the top of crumbling sections, and hopefully getting speed from gravity as they come down with the lip, to continue the ride.

Cutback

The point of surfing is to stay close to the curl, where the energy is greatest, and to surf in and around the curl to get the most out of a ride. Some waves are fast, or have flat spots, or the curl backs off for a moment, and that demands a **cutback** where the surfer speeds out onto the flat area at the end of a wave—also called the shoulder—and then re-directs speed to turn back to the curl.

Talk the Talk

A **roundhouse cutback** rebounds off the whitewater, to straighten out the turn to continue down the line.

A **layback cutback** was a move popular in the 1980s, where a surfer laid down on the wave during the cutback, and used body mass to slow it down to bring the board around.

Proper form on a respectable cutback: feet properly placed, hands not too high, foot on the tail to bring the board and body around, head pivoting to see where this cutback will go: all the way to the whitewater for a rebound or pull it up short.

A dedicated cutback, as seen from the shoulder. *Shutterstock*

Combinations

Turning combines all of the above basic turns into an ever-growing combination of turns, all of them designed to use speed and get more—but make it look good. Sometimes a top turn can also be a cutback.

In the twenty-first century, surfers like Dane Reynolds are using skateboard, snowboard, and other board sport techniques like 360s and aerials to increase the bag of tricks in ways the Hot Curl guys could never have imagined.

But 360 aerials and tail slides are advanced techniques. Best to get the basics down first: bottom turn, top turn, pump down the line, do a cutback.

A "double up" occurs when a larger wave moving faster overtakes a smaller wave. Sometimes their energy will combine, creating very fast sections that allow a surfer to pull into a "double-up barrel!" or turn through a "doubled-up section." This surfer is using the energy from the larger wave to drop into the smaller wave, and he is looking for a barrel. *Ocean Image Photography/Shutterstock*

Cruising on a perfect tropical wave, this surfer is exiting the previous section and wondering what the "end bowl" of this wave is going to do: barrel, taper, or close out. *Photogerson/Shutterstock*

WIPING OUT

Way back in the 1990s, World Champion surfer Martin Potter said: "If you can't have a spectacular ride, have a spectacular wipeout. It's good for the sport." Potter was kidding, kind of, and making a generation of surfers feel better when they went down big.

Surviving wipeouts can be fun in a kind of "Oh my God, I just escaped death or serious injury" adrenalized kind of way. It's a rush to fall from the top of a three-story wave, hit water that feels like concrete, get the wind knocked out of you, get picked up by several hundred tons of water, go over the falls at what feels like 100 miles an hour (160 kilometers per hour), and have that enormous amount of energy depth charge you 30 feet (9 meters) under water, where you roll around well past your lung capacity, lose track of what is up or down, nearly black out, see your life

The dictionary definition of a wipeout, illustrated. And wipeouts rarely get any more dramatic than here, at Pipeline. *Lucia Griggi*

Surviving Wipeouts

BROCK LITTLE DESCRIBES
ONE OF THE WORST WIPEOUTS EVER

Brock Little was one of the great dedicated big-wave surfers in the world from the 1980s through the 1990s. He grew up on the North Shore of Oahu, Hawaii, with Waimea Bay in his backyard. In his earliest days, he and his friends paddled out there as teenagers on big days to see who could wipeout the worst.

Brock soon got the hang of the place, and that lead to him being invited to the 1990 Quiksilver Big Wave Invitational in Honor of Eddie Aikau. This contest turned out to be a legendary event, as Waimea was about as big and perfect that day as it gets. There were two dozen of the world's best big-wave surfers on the beach, and a $55,000 first prize up for grabs. Anything was possible.

The wave Brock paddled into was a giant. He attempted it, but wiped out. And bad. That wipeout has gone down in surfing history as one of the worst ever.

These days, Brock is a top Hollywood stuntman, surfing his specialty. If you saw Live Free or Die Hard, *Brock is the second henchman killed by Bruce Willis.*

Brock spends most of his time in Hawaii and some of it in California, and he is sponsored by Hurley. Blogging for the Hurley website, this is how Brock described attempting—and surviving—what remains one of the biggest waves any mortal has paddled into with his bare hands.

"I'm best known for almost making the biggest wave ever paddled into. I didn't come close to making it, but it's an OK story . . . .

"The wave came during the 1990 Eddie Aikau. It was featured on last year's Eddie poster, and it's also been in and out of magazines for the last few decades. I won't tell the whole Eddie story, I'll save it for another column. I'll just talk about the wave.

"That day I was fearless. I had almost drowned a couple years before that day; I knew I could die, so I didn't want to fall. When that wave was coming I knew I would make it. The whole Waimea Bay was like a stadium. When that set hit the horizon the crowd started to go crazy. Horns were honking, people were yelling, and most of the people in my heat were paddling their ass off toward the middle of the ocean.

"One of my goals was to catch a closeout set before I got too old. This was my chance. I sat inside on the reef shelf and waited. The pack was twenty or thirty yards [18 or 27 meters] outside me, and they were still paddling out. [Fellow big-wave surfer Ken] Bradshaw was close to me but more on the shoulder. Aaron Napoleon was paddling out from catching a wave. I'd like to say I was calm as I waited, but the truth is I was full of butterflies . . . I cruised over the first wave of the set, and then saw the whole ocean stand up in front of me. The wave was coming right to me—I had to go. I turned around, put my head down, and started paddling. The hardest thing about riding the giants are catching them. You put everything you got into catching a beast of a wave, knowing it could kill you, but you do it anyway. Why?

"Aaron was one of my best friends growing up, and he was a good person to push me. As I paddled for the wave he was yelling, 'Go! Go! Go! You got it!' I looked over at Bradshaw—he was going, too. He stood up, but kinda pulled back on his feet. The wave was all mine. I knew I was going to make it. Half way down the face, something was going wrong, and I realized I was going to fall. Looking back, there was just too much water moving.

"I don't think I could have done anything better. That wave was not meant to be ridden. Maybe with a jet ski. Anyway, as I began falling, my life started to flash before my eyes. I don't think I'd even hit the water yet. My mom was carrying me, then I was running, stuff like that. When I almost drowned: I had an out-of-body experience, but I still don't believe in that kind of weird stuff.

"When I hit the wave it was like falling on concrete. Well, it wasn't that sore, but the water didn't let me penetrate. I kicked and flipped but I couldn't get into the wave. Thoughts about mom stopped. I worried about the lip falling on my body. I finally got into the wave, but not very deep. I was getting sucked over. As I was going over, I stuck my head out and got a breath. I'm not sure if I hallucinated seeing the whole bay, or really saw it, but I saw all the people and cars around the stadium.

"I was under water for a long time, but when you basically expect to die, it didn't really seem too bad. When I came to the surface, I think I was surprised to be alive. At that point I wasn't doing too well in the contest, so I went out and surfed the rest of my heat.

"When I came in people looked at me weird. It was like they were looking at a ghost. It was kinda cool. My mom told me my brother left, cause he didn't want to see me kill myself. Well I made it. . . . Wish I could have made the wave."

Cinderella versus Godzilla

JAY MORIARITY SURVIVES A BIG-WAVE WIPEOUT AT MAVERICK'S

It was a Cinderella story. Or perhaps, a Cinderella meets Godzilla story.

In December 1994, a 16-year-old Santa Cruz surfer named Jay Moriarity decided to surf one of the gnarliest big waves out there, the offshore break at Maverick's in northern California. At Pillar Point Harbor, Jay snagged a boat ride so he could get a look at the conditions. Maverick's was humungous. The biggest waves Jay had ever seen were bowling onto the reef, held up until the last minute by a 5.9 high tide and 20-knot offshore winds. The water is cold, the air even colder. There are 10 guys out surfing, including Evan Slater, Darryl Virostko, the Wormhoudt brothers, Alistair Kraft, Nacho Lopes, and Chris Brown. The sets are consistent, but few are being ridden. It is too big, too windy, and too high tide. Evan Slater paddles for a set, side-slips down the face, and bounces 3 feet (1 meter) in the air before going over the falls.

Jay paddles out soon after, passing people frozen by the weather, nerves, or both. He finds his lineup at the top of the bowl and waits no more than 10 minutes for a set to come through. He paddles for a set, gets to his feet—and is launched into big-wave history.

Ben Marcus: Were you out of your mind?

Jay Moriarity: I thought I had it. To me it looked good, but it turned out to be a nightmare.

Ben Marcus: What went wrong?

Jay Moriarity: I was a little too deep, but I feel like if the wind wasn't on it, I could have made it. Everything looked good as I was paddling for it and as I started to stand up, I thought: 'This will be a cool wave. It'll be fine.' I got to my feet and for a split second it felt OK. Then the whole wave ledged out and I could feel myself getting lifted by the wind. The wave went straight up and I had a moment to look down into a bottomless ocean. I had time to think, 'Oh shit. This is not good.' The next thing I knew, I was getting drilled.

Ben Marcus: How did you handle it?

Jay Moriarity: From what I've learned about wiping out, you just have to relax and let it beat the crap out of you and hope you come up. So I relaxed.

Ben Marcus: Did it hurt?

Jay Moriarity: Yeah, it hurt. The impact felt like I was

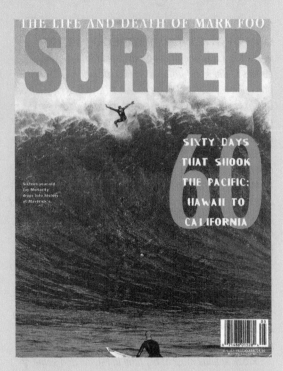

Surfer magazine cover showing Jay Moriarty at Maverick's.

getting hit by ten semi-trucks all at once. I was amazed by how hard it hit me, and I was amazed that it didn't rip me to pieces.

Ben Marcus: I've seen the video of that wave. From the time you fall into the lip until the time your head pops up in the whitewater it took twenty-one seconds.

Jay Moriarity: It felt like I was down there for years. The impact pushed me so deep I actually hit the bottom on my back. I was thinking, 'Wow, I've never heard of anyone hitting bottom out here. I hope I come up.' I somehow got my feet under me and pushed off. It seemed like it took me forever to get to the surface. I was stroking up and up with my eyes open, but it was completely black. It was black forever, then I could see a little light and I popped up.

Ben Marcus: Did you get close to panicking?

Jay Moriarity: When I was under I was thinking, 'If I don't get to the surface soon, I'll get hit by the second one for sure.' But I was calm. I was scared, but I wasn't going to panic. I came up a little dazed, but not gasping.

flash in front of your eyes, convert to several religions all at once, ask for deliverance, struggle to the surface—going toward the light—and surface to get half a lungful of air before the second wave of the set hits and does the same thing, all over again.

Surviving wipeouts like that is a rush, because it's a relief to be alive. But for the most part, wipeouts can be hazardous to children and other living things and are best to be avoided. Because:

1. Wiping out means you did something wrong on a wave and missed opportunities on a wave.
2. Wiping out can endanger your physical person, your surfboard, and the people around you.
3. Wiping out is embarrassing and could lead to public ridicule.
4. If other surfers see you wipeout often enough, you will be ignored and won't catch any more waves.

There are lots and lots of different ways to wipe out: You pearl on takeoff, flub your bottom turn or dig a rail on your top turn, or your cutback, or just going down the line. There are as many ways to wipeout as there are to make a wave. But most of them are best avoided, because wiping out can lead to injury to yourself and others, damage to equipment, or public embarrassment and social ostracization.

How to Wipeout—Correctly

When everything goes wrong, there are things to do right. Beginning surfers will be riding waves in shallow water, for the most part, and so it's important to remember a couple of things:

1. Dive shallow.
2. Always protect yourself.
3. Always protect your head.

Wiping out also leads to injury, and there is no part of your body that is safe: your head, nose, face, teeth, ribs, groin, legs, ankles, and feet are all fair game to the wipeout. If you ask surfers who have been around long enough about injuries, they will roll up a sleeve or hold their lips open with their fingers or part their hair and show off scars, chipped teeth, or some other souvenir of a wipeout.

Wipeouts are inevitable. They are going to happen when you are a rank beginner, and they happen to the world's best surfers. Here are some important things to remember about wipeouts: Know where you are. If you are falling and about to hit the water, it's important to know how deep it is below you and how close the falling lip is behind you. Sometimes it is essential to land deep and not penetrate the water, because sometimes there is not much water under the surface.

Other times you want to go as deep as you can in a wipeout to escape the lip that is descending right behind you with weight and force and maybe to get under the wave, swim out the back and avoid getting picked up and thrown over the falls.

SITTING ON TOP OF THE WORLD

The Beach Boys were onto something when they sang, "Catch a wave and you're sitting on top of the world." At some point in the surfing career of all beginners—or at least the ones who stick with it—there will come a moment when everything goes right: you paddle out properly with your hair dry, find the lineup, and wait for a good wave. There is no one behind you; the wave is yours. You paddle into it, angle the right way, and where you have done it wrong so many times before and flubbed it a hundred ways from Sunday, this time it all goes well.

From the island of Kauai, a place where watermen are watermen and even the women are gnarly, Keala Kennelly has been one of the bravest women pro surfers of the twenty-first century. She's not afraid to throw spray on a big turn or pull into the barrel at Teahupoo. Here, she rips a wave at Off The Wall, Hawaii. *Mana Photo/Shutterstock*

Paddle into the right spot, get to your feet in one motion, angle across the green water, and ride the wave, all the way to the end, no mistakes, a tiny bit of style, and then kick out in safe water.

Stoked.

It will happen. Sooner for some, later for others. At some point it's all going to come together. You are going to do it right, and it's a feeling that will never go away, and a feeling you will spend the rest of your life trying to recapture.

Catch a wave and sit on top of the world. It will put a hook into you and just like that, it's a lifetime obsession. And then it becomes a matter of more, more, more.

And getting more will become an extension of learning: frustrating at times, rewarding at others. Like any addiction, surfers develop a tolerance to thrills and are always on the lookout for something bigger and better: a longer wave, a hollower wave, a bigger wave, a more beautiful wave. Warmer, deeper, faster, stronger.

More, more, more.

The obsession can become so strong that a surfer moving up will make life changes to accommodate the vagaries of the ocean and the illusiveness of that next big thrill. Surfing can be as damaging as other addictions, but it's also a clean addiction, a healthy addiction, and the positives of catching waves should outweigh the negatives associated with investing time and money to get those waves.

The truth about learning to surf is that the learning curve never ends. Talk to the most experienced, talented surfers in the world, and they will tell you that no matter how many waves they have ridden, from tiny to giant, from Australia to Zanzibar, the desire for that thrill never ends, and the ocean has an undistinguishable ability to provide that thrill.

The horizon is the limit.

Health and Safety

NEVER TURN YOUR BACK on the ocean. Always treat it with respect, even on the smallest days, because the ocean is like a giant dragon tied up in your backyard. Just when you think you know all its moods, it will do something unpredictable and you will end up with a sliced foot, a reef rash up and down your back, or a broken nose, a black eye, a cracked noggin.

Or you'll just drown, and that will be the end of that.

Famous big-wave surfer Roger Erickson summed up the dangers of the ocean with one line: "Everything's okay until it isn't." And he was and is right. The ocean has drowned beginning surfers and it has drowned some of the most experienced, the fittest, and the most knowledgeable big-wave surfers.

Pro surfer Rochelle Ballard rides a backside barrel. *Karen Wilson*

Fearless

**PRO SURFER ROCHELLE BALLARD
DETAILS THE DAMAGE**

Rochelle Ballard was one of the most important women pro surfers from the 1990s and into the twenty-first century. A native of Kauai, Hawaii, she learned to surf at age 12, inspired by Margo Oberg, one of the pioneers of women's competitive surfing.

Rochelle grew up learning to charge powerful, shallow, dangerous waves. The Kauai attitude is that talk is cheap and actions speak louder, and that is why Kauai produces surfers who charge hard—men and women.

Rochelle turned professional in 1991 and through the 1990s and into the twenty-first century she was the leader of the pack of women, going deeper and gnarlier and leading the women's charge into waves that had long been considered the domain of men.

In her years as a surfer, Rochelle has had her triumphs, but she also paid her dues. Here is her account of just some of the injuries she has suffered: how she got them, how she recovered, and what she learned.

1. "During the filming of *Blue Crush*, I was medevaced and listed in critical condition during a stunt shoot. It was the scene where Anne Marie is cut off by her ex-boyfriend and they collide. I was surfing for Kate Bosworth and Chris Won was surfing for himself as the ex-boyfriend. We were out at perfect Lani's. First wave, riding down the line, I see cinematographer Don King set up for the shot, but no Chris. So I kicked out. At the same time that I was kicking out, Chris was trying to catch up and come down in front of me. I didn't see him and he didn't know I was going to kick out. He came down around me the same time I was kicking out and we collided so hard that both of us went flying. It was an instant slamming pain to my neck with his ass, and sudden paralysis to my left arm and neck. Water patrolman Brock Little rode in with the jet ski to pick me up and had to grab me out of the water. I couldn't get up myself. They sent me off in the medevac helicopter to Queens and put me under observation for a few hours. It was what they call in football, 'a stinger': temporary paralysis from the nerves being traumatized. I was off the set for two weeks, during which time the shoot had a permit to surf perfect six- to eight-foot [2- to 2½-meter] Pipe with no one out. I sat on the beach while Noah Johnson pulled into perfect barrels

in a wig and bikini. What an unbelievable feeling that was! I saw my dream come true without me in it. Took me a couple years to recover from the nerve damage in my neck. Funny enough Chris Won is now doing bio sync and works on me at home.

2. "When I rode for Swatch, they sent me to Italy to ride an artificial wave called the Bruticus Maximus on the top of the hill in Florence. It was gorgeous, riding at night with the stars above the statue of David and guys riding into the sky doing big airs and tricks. I was the only girl. It was an amazing setup: Big cranes with cameras hooked up panning across the wave, spotlights, music, and crazy riding. I was having a hard time with it. I kept getting pitched over the barrel and slammed against the back wall right when I'd get back into the green room. Christian Fletcher felt bad, so he told me to jump on his back on the bodyboard and stand up on him when we got in the barrel. I finally was riding in the barrel, everyone was cheering. We were in it for a while, and didn't know one of the riders was standing above the barrel on the frame. He didn't see that we were still in the wave and jumped from the top and landed right on my head and shoulders. It worked me! Everyone was tripping. I went home that night with an amazingly sore neck and a swollen bruised ass! They never got me back to the Bruticus Maximus again. I was over it. The boyz can have that one.

3. "The 1997 US Open at Huntington Beach, California, was held during a bombing south swell. It was four to six feet [1 to 2 meters], big current, and closeout lefts into the pier. In the semifinals, I caught a left toward the pier, kicked out, and behind that was a big set. I was too far away from the pier to paddle through it. I duck dove a wave and got a little closer to the pier. The next wave came and I was stuck in a really bad spot. If I tried to duck it, it could slam me backside into a pier piling. So I turned round and straightened out to try and dodge through the pilings: *baaaaaad* move. I dodged one piling and hit the next one head on! The whitewash was so big it lifted me up above the water level about four feet [1 meter] (which was a good thing considering the lower area on the piling was full of barnacles that could have sliced me up. Yikes!). I hit smack-dab on the left side of my forehead, instantly saw stars and passed out for a couple

Rochelle Ballard displays her injuries. *John Bilderback*

seconds. Pam Burridge was paddling out on the other side of the pier and saw it happen. She instantly grabbed me. I came to and immediately got on my board and tried to paddle back out. Pam was like: 'What are you doing? The shore is the other way! You need to get in! You hit the pier! You're not OK!' There were a couple minutes left and I was so determined to make it through the heat, I wasn't even aware that I came as close as it gets to being paralyzed, permanent brain damage, or death. I just wanted to get to the finals. Pam helped me to the shore. It wasn't until I set foot on the sand and was immediately surrounded by lifeguards and paramedics that it all hit me. I had the biggest bump on my forehead. My ex, Dad, Grandma, and Lisa Andersen were all standing over me tripping out and in tears. I think that's what scared me more. I was like: If they're crying, I must be in pretty critical condition. I started to panic and passed out a couple times. Somehow I woke up the next morning watching the news and saw a special about head trauma, and all the things that can happen. I was drinking a cup of coffee while icing my head and feeling pretty OK. It put me in such a big appreciation place that nothing worse happened to me. They postponed the contest until that next day, just in case I was well enough to surf. So I decided to do it. My family was not too happy about my decision, but I was amped. I won the contest and the next WCT in Lacanau. It took about four years of chronic headaches and neck pain until I recovered.

4. "When I was fourteen, the nose of my board hit me in the face, on the right side of my nose and fractured my right orbital rim. I had to get surgery and a tiny plate put in. It was one-foot [30-centimeter] waves and poor surfing. Just a fluke.

5, 6, 7. "I broke my nose three different times until I finally had reconstructive surgery on it. The first time was on Kauai when I was sixteen. I pulled into a closeout barrel and when I fell off, it tossed me straight to the bottom and I banged my nose on a flat rock. The second time, Serena Brooke and I were playing footy on the beach at Logs. She tackled me and her knee accidentally hit my nose. The third time was at Tavarua. They had just put in the epic swimming pool. I had some kava and was super floaty. I dove into the pool and took a couple strokes and bumped my nose into a shelf that you couldn't see at night unless you knew it was there. So, my nose was not very cute any more. I had it straightened soon after.

8. "I went surfing with Bruce Irons, Andy Irons, and Keala Kennelly when I was twenty-two. We were out on the north side of Kauai surfing a barreling left. I pulled into a closeout and got sent straight to the bottom. My head and shoulder hit the reef . . . I was so shook up by it. They cleaned me up and calmed me down. I was afraid of surfing backside barrels for a few years after that. I was afraid of hitting my head again. It wasn't until Teahupoo became an event for us that I really started enjoying my backside barrel riding.

9. "During the filming for an O'Neill surf movie in Tahiti, I hit my head in a closeout, solid six-foot [1¾-meter] west bowl. I was surfing with Shane Beschen, Cory Lopez, and Jay Moriarity. It was six- to eight-foot [2- to 2½-meter] Teahupoo and pretty nuts. I was pretty nervous. I had been catching some great waves for the last couple days when it was four to six feet [2 meters]. Today was way heavier. I took off on the first wave of a big set. I grabbed my rail on the drop and then let go and stood up in the barrel. It was so big and round. I realized a second later I wasn't going to make it out. At the time, I didn't have enough experience out there to realize it was better to jump off than keep riding it through, because it only gets more shallow. So I rode it through until the foamball lifted and tossed me off my board. I went under and before I could control my body in the turmoil, it took me and threw me over with the lip. I had this horrible feeling I was going to hit. The instant I hit the surface, my head slammed on the reef. I came up dizzy with blood pouring out of my head. I was on dry reef at this point with sets still coming and an enormous amount of whitewash heading straight for me. The only chance I had of not being cheese-grated on the reef was to belly-ride the board straight in. Usually when that big of a whitewash comes through and you try to belly it, you get creamed. Somehow, the angels were looking after me and I made it to the lagoon. I was taken to the emergency room and the doctor came in with shorts, a T-shirt, and no shoes. He cleaned it up and said he couldn't stitch it, because it was a little hole not a gash. I don't willingly pull into closeouts at Chopes anymore.

10. "We were filming for the original *Blue Crush* all-girls surf video in Samoa. Salani's was about six to eight feet [2 to 2½ meters] and pretty thick. After kicking out of a wave, a bomb broke right in front of me. I tried to duck dive it, but the board ripped out of my hand and my leash snapped off and the board got tossed into the cliffside. The wave grabbed me like a dog with a piece of meat and ravished me. I tore my intercostal muscles, in between my shoulder blades and ribs. Salani's is a good distance from the shore, about a fifteen-minute paddle out. There I was: no board, torn muscles, and I had to swim in. That sucked! Took me a while to heal from that one. Paddling was too painful. I skipped the Gunston 500 in Durban, South Africa, a couple months later.

11. "I was out at Sunset, Hawaii, dropping into a twelve-foot [3½-meter] wave. I hit a bump and got launched forward. I was going so fast that it skipped me down the face and I fractured a rib, just above my chest.

12. "I pulled into a barrel out at Backdoor, Hawaii, the foamball caught up with me, tossed me, and the nose of my board spun around and jabbed me in the ribs. It fractured one under my right chest.

13. "When I was thirteen, I hit the reef with my right knee surfing a shallow left at home. I had to get seven stitches.

14. "When I was growing up, I pulled into a sandbar barrel backside at home. The foamball caught up with me and flipped my board up, tossed me around. The fin sliced my right foot. I got seven stitches in the foot.

15. "I have a Junior Pro contest that I started on Kauai in the summer of 2004. The day that the kids were all coming in for the camp I went out for an evening session at my local break. It was a bombing south swell. I was on the outside left. It was five to six feet [1½ to 2 meters] with some eight-foot [2½-meter] drainers. I was having one of those easy sessions, good timing, avoiding the big impact sections, and having fun. This spot usually doesn't barrel, but it was kegging that day! It looked like a mini Chopes. I hooked under the lip in a fat pit, grabbed my rail, and locked in. Right when I could feel the spit ride up my backside, the foamball lifting my tail up and the vision of an opening was coming, the wave hit a weird water pocket and the wall of water over the top of me clammed down on me like a can being smashed. I felt my right foot touch my shin and my whole leg shove up into my hip. I was in so much pain; it put me in a state of panic, like I couldn't swim. I quickly snapped out of it, realizing if I didn't I could be in a worse situation with sets rolling in over me. I got on my board and belly-rode in. My friends were there to carry me up and take me to the hospital. I tore, compressed, and stretched my ligaments, muscles, and tendons and hairline fractured my anklebones. Heavy! I had sixty-five kids show up that same night to surf with me at my camp and compete in the contest and I was on crutches. Even worse, I was sitting in fourth on the WCT two weeks before the Malibu event.

16. "This is after I twisted my ankle in a big barrel in summer 2005. Four months later, I was finally able to surf without tape on my foot. I was on Kauai with Keala Kennelly riding a PWC. Keala and I just started riding together and learning to drive and whip each other in. We were riding a wave through on the inside checking the surf. There isn't a channel at this spot. It was closing out on a sandbar. The wave we were riding shut down and the whitewash was dissipating. Suddenly it reformed. We were close to the shore, but I thought I could just ride over the top. Our boards were in the gunnels, in between our feet. We got bumped around in the whitewash and pushed to the shore. When we were on the shore trying to push the PWC off the shorebreak, I realize I had broken my left foot. It was pretty scary. The surf wasn't big, but the PWC is and we were out there by ourselves. We were tripping. I broke it in two places on the same metatarsal bone—six weeks before the first contest of the season. I went through some intense therapy to heal faster. Bones usually take six to eight weeks for recovery. Then you can be physical. That meant no walking, up until the start of the contest. That's just to walk, forget about surfing. I didn't cast it to save less recovery time from muscle regeneration. I was spending hours in a hyperbaric oxygen chamber, getting acupuncture, and massage. It was two weeks before the first event and I was nowhere near healed. The bone was still not connected. It broke in two spots on the same bone. So, I flew to California and saw Kent Ewing and my brother and received bio sync. It's bodywork that unwinds the muscle tissue with chi energy and brings blood flow back into the area. I also did a treatment with a magnet machine that is supposed to grow bones faster. Within one week, I started to walk. It was painful, but I was walking. I started surfing four days before the Roxy Pro at Snapper started. I made it to the semi-finals.

EPILOGUE

What good is life unless you experience it, live in the moment, and take your challenges at whatever level that may be, big or small.

From the earliest years of surfing until the 1990s, no famous surfer had ever been killed while surfing. And then, beginning in 1993, it was four in a row: On December 23, 1994, Hawaiian surfer Mark Foo flew to California to try Maverick's—an upstart big-wave spot that was challenging all the Hawaiian waves for the title of World's Gnarliest Wave. Surfing a big but not huge day under almost perfect conditions, Foo took a wipeout that didn't look too bad, and no one noticed when he didn't surface. Maverick's is a big place offshore, with a lot going on. Later in the day, a boat of surfers returning to the harbor found Foo's body floating just beneath his surfboard. He might have gotten trapped under water in a cave, under a ledge, or maybe his leash pinned him. Maybe the force of the wave knocked him out. Foo was one of the best big-wave surfers in the world, and he drowned.

Almost a year to the day later, when other surfers paddled out into Waimea Bay, Hawaii, in a tribute to Mark Foo, California surfer Donnie Solomon drowned when he went over the falls backward. Solomon got caught inside a big set, and he was paddling out in the path of local Hawaiian surfer Kawika Stant. Solomon could have bailed his board and dove through, but he obeyed the protocol, tried to push through the wave, and went over the falls backward. And he drowned.

In 1997, Hawaiian surfer Todd Chesser was on Maui where he was supposed to stage a stunt for the end of the movie *Riding Giants*. Chesser was being paid to go over the falls at Jaws and pretend to drown. For mysterious reasons, he left Maui and returned to Oahu, where a giant swell was predicted. Some say Chesser went home to spend Valentine's Day with his *wahine*, others knew that Chesser did not approve of the use of personal watercraft in big surf, and he left because he wanted no part in a movie that used the machines. Back on Oahu, Chesser paddled to an outside reef called Alligator Rock with two friends, Aaron Lambert and Cody Graham.

The three surfers got caught inside a sneaker set, and Chesser drowned. Lambert and Graham nearly drowned, and they spent the next hour swimming their dead friend in from the outside reef to the inner reef. The double irony in all of this is that if there had been a PWC around, Chesser would have survived.

In 1994, 16-year-old Jay Moriarity survived a tremendous wipeout at Maverick's that was many orders of magnitude worse than the wipeout that killed Mark Foo. Jay's wipeout made the cover of *Surfer* magazine and launched Jay as a surf star. Seven years later, Jay was in the Maldive Islands, training for big-wave hold downs by swimming to the bottom of the ocean and sitting there in a sort of yoga trance—training his body to burn oxygen slowly. Something went wrong, and Jay Moriarity drowned.

After 50 years of no deaths, four of the world's most experienced surfers drowned within a decade. These guys were physically fit, they knew what they were doing, and the ocean still got them.

Let that be a caveat to anyone and everyone entering the ocean. Never turn your back. Always protect yourself. The ocean is beautiful, but it is dangerous.

Talk the Talk

Wahine is Hawaiian term of affection for women surfers.

Rochelle Ballard's Secret Weapon: The Sambazon Acai Smoothie

ACCORDING TO PRO SURFER Rochelle Ballard, "This is the Ferrari of Sambazon Acai Smoothies!"

Ingredients
1 Sambazon acai pack
1 handful fresh blueberries
1 banana
¼ cup nuts of your choice
   (I prefer macadamias and walnuts)
1 medium mango or papaya (or your local seasonal fruit)
2 tablespoons shredded coconut
1½ cups Zico coconut water (use more for a more liquidy shake or less for a thicker acai bowl)
2 tablespoons of any good source of enzyme-based protein powder with veggies, fruit, omegas, chlorophyll, and greens
¼ cup Swiss Chard or spinach

Rochelle Ballard and her secret weapon.

ROCHELLE SAYS: "Eating a balanced diet without junk food, processed food, and excess sugars is a way for the body to heal itself. Antioxidants from things like acai, berries, fruit, coconut water, and veggies is what keeps inflammation down and helps prevents cancer. Toxins are what ages the brain and tissue. Drinking a good amount of water hydrates your body and flushes the system. Protein is great for long-term energy

"When you have any of the 'instant satisfaction' stuff, that isn't enhancing for your system, especially a night out with drinks. Coconut water, acai, berries, and lots of water is a great way to replenish your system. We all like to over indulge, but it's rebuilding the system that makes the difference."

Protect Your Head

Skylar Peake is a 24-year-old waterman and surf instructor from Malibu.

"Learning how to fall in the ocean is vital to a successful and relatively painless surfing experience. Protecting your body and specifically your head when you fall must become second nature to those that surf. No matter how much experience you have, there is still going to be a time where your board whacks you and you get hurt.

"My name is Skylar Peak and I have been surfing since I was five. I scored my first head injury from a surfboard fin at age ten while in a National Scholastic Surfing Association contest at Jalama Beach, California. I took a fin to the left cheek and still wear a scar from it today—fifteen years later.

"I have taught surfing for ten years, and one of the most important things I do is show people how to cover their head. The key is: Know your environment and swell conditions and be aware of where your board is when you fall. This will help you avoid collisions with your board.

"When you fall in deep water, fall away from your board and allow your body to penetrate the water. By going down deeper, you will avoid a collision with your board. The wave energy passes over you, and you avoid the Washing Machine Effect, where you can often collide with your board.

Beware of Your Own Surfboard

Know your environment, the swell conditions, and be aware of where your surfboard is when you fall. This will all help you avoid collisions with your board.

"When falling in shallower water, fall away from your board and spread out your surface area over the water so you do not penetrate deep and hit the bottom. If you think you are going to hit the bottom, it is a good idea to get into a ball so you can bounce. Wrap your arms around the back of your head. You would much rather bounce your arms than your head off of the reef or a sand bar.

"It is also important not to jump off your board with straight or locked legs in shallow water. The impact with the bottom in shallow water can cause severe knee or ankle injury.

"A surfer friend of mine, Jesse Billauer, hit his head on the sandbar at Westward Beach, California, in 1996 and was left a quadriplegic. While this was a freak accident and Jesse was a very experienced surfer, I cannot stress how important it is to protect your neck and head from injury. You can do so by putting your hands out in front of your head when you dive under a wave and not falling head first into the bottom.

"Most collision-related injuries with a board result in a laceration from a fin or a bruise. I would prefer a bruised arm instead of a lacerated skull any day of the week. You can cover your head by putting your arms over your head and making a protective 'X' with your arms—all the while tucking your chin down to your chest. Every wave is different and no two times you fall are the same, but I encourage you to be aware of your environment and keep your head protected all the time.

"It is also important to have a properly sized leash so that the recoil does not fling the board at you after you fall. A leash should typically be four to twelve inches [10 to 30 centimeters] longer than your board. In larger waves, your leash will stretch more, adding to the speed at which your board will recoil back at you. Also, a thinner leash will stretch more and also have more recoil.

"It is important to cover your head not only when you fall into the water, but to cover it when you come up after a fall. Often, your board gets launched in the air if you pearl—or simply by the force of a wave—and the leash connected to your ankle will pull the board at you.

"In 2005, I was on a boat trip in Indonesia and took a fin to the head on the smallest wave of the trip that left me knocked out. I woke up when the next wave hit me and had a severe laceration that split my left ear in two.

Skylar Peak protects his delicate head—and his expensive paddle—in a wipeout while standup paddle surfing. *Dave Collyer*

The Washing Machine Effect

The Washing Machine Effect is caused by the swirl of the wave spinning the water, your board, and yourself around.

The recoil from the leash pulled the board at me and ended my trip. I simply wasn't expecting it. After a ten-hour boat ride back to Padang and a two-hour flight, I had to get surgery in Singapore before returning to the United States. Not a fun experience, but nevertheless covering your head in small waves is just as important as when the waves are big.

"You can never let your guard down in the ocean."

Jack Gets Cracked

Even if you grow up at a surf spot and know it like your own backyard because it *is* your own backyard, it will still get you. That is what happened to Jack Johnson at Pipeline, when his ambition was pro surfing.

That wipeout rearranged Jack's face temporarily, but it also changed the course of his life. If it wasn't for that "Pipe wipe," Jack's soundtrack to the movie *Curious George* wouldn't have been as good.

Born on the North Shore in 1975 to surfing parents and surfing brothers, Jack grew up on the beach at Pipeline—which is a little like having a Tyrannosaurus Rex chained in the backyard. Jack first surfed Pipeline when he was 10 years old. He grew up knowing Pipeline inside out. But it still bit him.

In 1992, Jack was 17 years old when he made the local trials of the Pipeline Masters—a major accomplishment for a Hawaiian kid. Two weeks later, Jack wiped out at Pipeline, hit the reef, and came up missing teeth and needing 150 stitches in his head. During his two-month recovery, Jack worked on his music and decided to turn away from pro surfing and go to the University of California–Santa Barbara to study film.

Johnson graduated from UCSB with a film degree in 1997. In 1998, he produced the surf movie *Thicker Than Water* with the Malloys—surfing brothers from Ventura, California, who had also taken their lumps at Pipeline, especially Chris, who is still famous for a head-first over the falls pile driver that appeared in *Surfing* magazine sometime in the 1990s. While working on *Thicker Than Water*, Jack recorded a song with G. Love for the soundtrack. In 2002, Jack and Kelly Slater produced the surf movie *September Sessions*, and that same year, Jack was encouraged by Ben Harper and his producer JP Plunier to record *Brushfire Fairytales*. The album went platinum, and was followed by *On and On* in 2003, which sold more than a million copies.

It is unlikely any of that would have happened if Jack hadn't nearly wiped his face on the reef at Pipeline in 1992. His mother still can't believe how rich or famous her son is: "I thought you wanted to be a pro surfer!" she still tells him.

YOGA FOR SURFING
Pro Surfer Rochelle Ballard says:

"Finding a balance in life and becoming more aware of how you feel becomes a choice that many of us choose to make. That is what is so amazing about yoga, surfing, and wellness. When I'm out surfing for hours pushing my body or having a stressful day, yoga helps to flush out the toxins, rejuvenates my body, stimulates the joints, muscles, and relieves tension and pain.

"Doing yoga on a regular basis strengthens your core, muscles, and elongates your body and overall posture, creating more energy and resilience, preventing injury, and a youthful life.

"Tuning into my breathing eliminates stress, quiets the mind chatter, helps me overcome fear, gives me energy, and makes me smile, laugh, and enjoy life more."

Rochelle Ballard does yoga, beachside.

Sun Salutation: Forward bend, downward dog, plank, upward dog.
Benefits for surfing: Tones your muscles, strengthens the upper, lower back, arms, legs, feet, and builds your core strength in the deep abdominal muscles. Lengthens your spine and stretches your hamstrings, hip flexors, and opens your chest. All of this increases awareness of your body and mind.

Bridge Pose
Benefits for surfing: Stretches
the neck, strengthens the
muscles in the butt, back, and
hamstrings, rejuvenating tired
legs. Creates more powerful
turns and leg strength and
improves balance.

Camel Pose
Benefits for surfing: Opens the chest, pecs, shoulders, and arms. Great after a long session of paddling. It also strengthens the buttocks and opens the hip flexors

Leg, Hip Opener, Belly, and Spinal Twist
Benefits for surfing: Increases flexibility in your hips and legs, allowing for agility in your turns, preventing injury through the knees, low back, and lengthening and hydrating the spine.

Standing Poses
Benefits for surfing: Increases leg strength, improves your balance, coordination, and stabilizes your core. All of this makes for stronger surfing, less falling, and more fun.

Qigong cultivates the vital energy, life force, and breathe within you. Practicing qigong and yoga on a regular basis will keep us fit, full of energy, youthful, and healthy through out our lives.

Meditation and breathing is what sustains your body, eliminates stress, anxiety, and fear. It builds your vital energy, and directs your energy and focus to create and feel the things you desire in your life. Go get shacked, throw some tail, and live life to thrive not survive. Namaste!

Beginner Beaches and Surfing Schools Worldwide

THIS LIST INCLUDES many of the best surfing schools and beginner surf spots around the United States and the globe. This is by no means a complete list of the best places to learn to surf, but it's a good place to start.

Malibu, California, is one of the world's most famed surf spots. *Lucia Griggi*

HAWAIIAN ISLANDS
Waikiki Beach, South Shore, Oahu
Waikiki Beach is lined with surf shops, board rental kiosks, and professional beach boys trained, ready, and willing to take you to surfing. But the place Adam Sandler swears by is:
Hans Hedemann Surf
www.hhsurf.com

Launiupoko, Maui
Goofy Foot Surf School
www.goofyfootsurfschool.com

Maui Surfer Girls
www.mauisurfergirls.com

Hanalei, North Shore, Kauai
Hanalei Surf
www.hanaleisurf.com

CALIFORNIA
Linda Mar, Pacifica
Nor Cal Surf Shop
www.norcalsurfshop.com

Cowell's Beach, Lighthouse Point, Santa Cruz
Richard Schmidt School of Surfing
www.richardschmidt.com

Club Ed
www.club-ed.com

Mondos, Faria Point, Ventura County
Santa Barbara Surf School
www.santabarbarasurfschool.com

Surfclass.Com
www.surfclass.com

Soul Octopus
www.souloctopus.com

Surfrider Beach, Malibu
Carla Rowland Surf Instruction
www.carlarowland.com

Zuma Jays Surf Shop
www.zumajays.com

John Philbin
www.johnphilbin.com

San Onofre State Park, San Clemente
Paskowitz Surf Camp
www.paskowitz.com

Tourmaline Surfing Park, San Diego
Pacific Beach Surf School
www.pacificbeachsurfschool.com

La Jolla Shores, La Jolla
Surf Diva
www.surfdiva.com

OREGON
Ossie Surf Shop
www.ossiessurfshop.com

Lincoln City Surf Shop
www.lcsurfshop.com

CANADA
Frank Island, Tofino, British Columbia
Surf Sister
www.surfsister.com

TEXAS
South Padre Island
South Padre Surf Company
www.southpadresurfcompany.com

Galveston
Surf Specialties
www.surfspecialties.com

FLORIDA
Cocoa Beach
Ron Jon Surf Shop
www.ronjons.com

The Goods Surf And Skate
www.thegoodsshop.com

VIRGINIA

Virginia Beach
Wave Riding Vehicles
www.waveridingvehicles.com

17th Street Surf Shop
www.17thst.com/surfcamp.html

Titus International
www.titus-international.com

Billabong Camp
www.billabongcamps.com

SOUTH CAROLINA

Folly Beach
Ocean Surf Shop
www.oceansurfshop.com

McKevlins
www.mckevlins.com

NORTH CAROLINA

Outer Banks
Corolla Surf Shop
www.corollasurfshop.com

Wrightsville Beach
Sweet Water Surf Shop
www.sweetwatersurfshop.com

MARYLAND

Ocean City
Billabong Camps:
OC Groms Surf School
www.kcoast.com

NEW JERSEY

Sea Isle City
Heritage Surf and Sport
www.heritagesurf.com

NEW YORK

Robert Moses State Park
The Surf School
www.thesurfschool.com

Bunger Surf Shop
www.bungersurf.com

MASSACHUSETTS

Nantucket
Force 5 Watersports

Nantucket Island Surf School
www.surfack.com

Nantucket Surfari Surf Camp
www.nantucketsurfari.com

Coast Guard Beach,
Cape Cod National Seashore
Pump House Surf Co.
www.pumphousesurf.com

Nauset Sports
www.nausetsports.com

RHODE ISLAND

Narragansett Town Beach
Gansett Juice
www.gansettjuice.com

NEW HAMPSHIRE

Jenness Beach, Rye
Cinnamon Rainbows
www.cinnamonrainbows.com

MAINE

Oqunquit
Liquid Dreams
www.liquiddreamssurf.com

York
Liquid Dreams
www.liquiddreamssurf.com

MICHIGAN

New Buffalo
Third Coast Surf Shop
www.thirdcoastsurfshop.com

AUSTRALIA

Noosa Head, Queensland
Learn to Surf—Noosa
www.learntosurf.com.au

Noosa Surf Lessons
www.noosasurflessons.com.au

Currumbin Beach, Gold Coast, Queensland
Surf Easy
www.surfeasy.com.au

**Greenmount Beach, Coolangatta,
Gold Coast, Queensland**
Walkin' on Water
www.walkinonwater.com

Surfer's Paradise, Gold Coast, Queensland
Cheyne Horan Surf School
www.cheynehoran.com.au

Surf in Paradise
www.surfinparadise.com.au

Rainbow Bay, Gold Coast, Queensland
Gold Coast Learn To Surf Centre
www.goldcoastsurfingcentre.com

Byron Bay, New South Wales
Style Surfing
www.stylesurfingbyronbay.com

Sunrise Surfing Bryon Bay
www.sunrisesurfing.com

**South Palm Beach, Sydney,
New South Wales**
Matt Grainger's Palm Beach Surf School
www.surfschools.com/page41.html

Manly, Sydney, New South Wales
Manly Surf School
www.manlysurfschool.com

Cronulla, Sydney, New South Wales
Cronulla Surfing Academy
www.cronullasurfingacademy.com

Fisherman's Beach, Torquay, Victoria
Torquay Surfing Academy
www.torquaysurf.com.au

Australia's golden Gold Coast. *Treasure Dragon /Shutterstock*

Torquay Main Beach, Victoria
Southern Exposure Surf School
www.surfschools.com/page102.html

**Scarborough Beach, Perth,
Western Australia**
Learn to Surf—Perth
http://www.surfschool.com

Perth Go Surf
www.academyofsurfing.com/
schools-scarborough.html

BARBADOS
Surfer's Point
Zed's Surfing Adventures
www.zedssurftravel.com

Surfer's Point Guest House
www.surferspointbarbados.com

BRAZIL
Itacare, Bahia
Easy Drop Surf Camp
www.easydrop.com

Rio de Janeiro
Pedro Muller Starpoint Surf Club
www.escolapedromuller.com.br

Escola Carioca de Surf
www.escolacariocadesurf.com.br

Florianopolis
Surf School Evandro Santos
www.surfschoolbrazil.com

Nexus Brazil Surf Experience
www.nexussurf.com

CANARY ISLANDS
Fuerteventura
Quiksilver Surf School
www.quiksilver-surfschool.com

Lanzarote
Calima Surf Lanzarote
www.calimasurf.com

Surf School Lanzarote
www.surfschoollanzarote.com

Students at the Nexus Surf School in Florianopolis, Brazil, prepare to hit the water. *Courtesy Nexus Surf School*

United Surf Camps—
Surfcamp Lanzarote
www.unitedsurfcamps.com

Gran Canaria
United Surf Camps—
Surfcamp Gran Canaria
www.unitedsurfcamps.com

CHILE
Arica
Soul Rider Surf Camp—Arica
www.soulridercamp.com

United Surf Camps—Surfcamp Chile
www.unitedsurfcamps.com

Pichilemu
Pichilemu Institute
of Language Studies
www.pichilemulanguage.com

Vina del Mar
Chile Surf Camp & Trip
www.chilesurfcamp.cl

COSTA RICA
Jaco Beach/Playa Hermosa
Del Mar Surf Camp
www.costaricasurfingchicas.com

Nosara
Safari Surf School
www.safarisurfschool.com

Playa Dominical
Costa Rica Surf Camp
www.crsurfschool.com

Green Iguana Surf Camp
www.greeniguanasurfcamp.com

Playa Guiones, Nicoya Peninsula
Corky Carroll's Surf School—
Costa Rica
www.surfschool.net

Tamarindo
Costa Rica Surf Club
www.costaricasurfclub.com

Tamarindo Surf School
www.tamarindosurfschool.com

Tamarindo/Witch's Rock
Blue Trailz Surf Camp
www.bluetrailz.com

ENGLAND
**Sedgewell Cove, Bigbury-on-Sea,
South Devon**
Discovery Surf School
www.discoverysurf.com

Newquay, Cornwall
Rip Curl English Surfing Federation
www.englishsurfschool.com

Errant Surf School
www.errantsurfschool.com

Reef Surf School
www.reefsurfschool.com

Escape Surf School
www.escapesurfschool.co.uk

Quiksilver Surf School—Newquay
http://quiksilvernewquay.com

Polzeath, Cornwall
Surfs Up Surf School
www.surfsupsurfschool.com

Croyde, North Devon
Surfing Croyde Bay
www.surfingcroydebay.co.uk

ECUADOR
Montanita
Casa del Sol Surf Tours
www.casadelsolmontanita.com

FIJI
Tavarua Island
www.tavarua.com

Namotu Island
www.namotuislandfiji.com

FRANCE

Biarritz
Nomad Surfers Surfing Holidays—
Biarritz Surf Camp, School and Tours
www.nomadsurfers.com

Hossegor
The Natural Surf Lodge
www.naturalsurflodge.com

Nomad Surfers Surfing Holidays—
Hossegor Surf House, Camp and School
www.nomadsurfers.com

Lacanau
Aola Surf School
www.aolasurfschool.com

Bo and Co Surf Lessons
www.bocosurf.com

Seignosse
Seignosse Surf School
www.seignosse-surf-school.com

GHANA

Busua, Western Region
United Surf Camps—Surfcamp Ghana
www.unitedsurfcamps.com

INDONESIA

Kuta Beach
Rip Curl School of Surf
www.ripcurlschoolofsurf.com

Costa Rica's Playa Nosara, home of Safari Surf School.
Soul Arch Photography

Pro Surf School—Bali
www.prosurfschool.com/index.htm

Bukit Peninsula
Padang Padang Surf Camp
www.balisurfingcamp.com

Roti, Timor
Nemberala Beach Resort
www.nemberalabeachresort.com

IRELAND
Bundoran
TurfNSurf Lodge and Surf School
www.turfnsurf.ie

Bundoran Surf Co.
www.bundoransurfco.com

Surf Coach Ireland
www.surfcoachireland.ie

JAPAN
Kugenuma Beach, Shonan
T-Stick Surf Shop by the Sea Surfing School
www.t-sticksurf.com

MEXICO
Cabo San Lucas
Mike Doyle Surf School
www.cabosurfshop.com

Barras de Piaxtla, Mazatlan, Sinaloa
Nomad Surfers Surfing Holidays—Sinaloa
Surfcamp, Surf School and Accommodation
www.nomadsurfers.com

Playa Troncones, Zihuatenejo
Instructional Surf Adventures Mexico
www.isamexico.com

Mazatlan/Puerto Vallarta
East Pacific Surf Camp
www.eastpacsurf.com

Punta de Mita, Nayarit
Tranquilo Surf Adventures & Surf School
www.tranquilosurf.com

Puerto Escondido
Mexico Surf School
www.mexicosurfschool.com

MOROCCO
Taghazoute, Agadir
Surf Maroc
www.surfmaroc.co.uk

Surf Berbere
www.surfberbere.com

Pure Blue Water
www.purebluewater.com

NEW ZEALAND
Auckland
New Zealand Surf 'N' Snow Tours
www.newzealandsurftours.com

Mount Maunganui
New Zealand Surf School
www.nzsurfschools.co.nz

Raglan
Raglan Surfing School—New Zealand
www.raglansurfingschool.co.nz

NICARAGUA
Northern Nicaragua
Surf Tours Nicaragua—Surf Camps
www.surftoursnicaragua.com

Jiquilillo, Northern Nicaragua
Monty's Jiquilillo Surf Camp
www.nicaraguasurfbeach.com

Rancho Santana, Tola
The Surf Sanctuary
www.thesurfsanctuary.com

San Juan Del Sur, Rivas
Nicaragua Surf Report Surf School
nicaraguasurfreport.com

Playa Gigante, Rivas, southern Nicaragua
Giant's Foot Surf—Nicaragua
www.giantsfoot.com

PANAMA
Morro Negrito
Panama Surf Camp
www.panamasurfcamp.com

Playa Rio Mar, San Carlos
Río Mar Surf and Skate Camp
www.riomarsurf.com

Bocas del Toro
Azucar Surf
www.azucarsurf.com

Bocas del Toro Surf School
www.bocassurfschool.com

PERU
Playa Negra/Punta Hermosa
Calima Surf—Surf School Peru
www.surfcampholidays.com/peru_surfing/
surfcamp/surfschool_peru.php

North, Little North, Lima, Little South
Peru Surf Guides
www.perusurfguides.com

Little South/Lima
Olas Peru Surf Travel
www.olasperusurftravel.com

PORTUGAL
Figueira da Foz
Escola de Surf
www.surfingfigueira.com

Peniche
Peniche Surf Camp
www.penichesurfcamp.com

Baleal Surf Camp—Quiksilver
www.balealsurfcamp.com

Ericeira, Mafra, Lisbon Coast
Na Onda Surf School
www.ericeirasurf.com

Lagos, Algarve
Surf Experience
www.surf-experience.com

Nomad Surfers Surfing Holidays—
Carrapateira Surfcamp, Surf School
and Surfaris
www.nomadsurfers.com

PUERTO RICO
Rincon
Surf 787
www.surf787.com

Rincon Surf and Board
www.surfandboard.com

Isla Verde, Pine Grove
Puerto Rico Surf School
www.gosurfpr.com

SOUTH AFRICA
Muizenberg, Cape Town
Learn 2 Surf
www.learn2surf.co.za

Gary's Surf School
www.garysurf.com

Surf Shack
www.surfshack.co.za

Jeffreys Bay, Eastern Cape
Surf Masters Surf School
www.jeffreysbaytourism.org

Wavecrest Surf School
www.jeffreysbaytourism.org

Ubuntu Jeffreys Bay Surf School
www.jaybay.co.za

United Surf Camps—
Surf Camp South Africa
www.unitedsurfcamps.com

Port Elizabeth, Eastern Cape
Learn 2 Surf—Port Elizabeth
www.learn2surf.co.za

East London, Eastern Cape
Learn 2 Surf—East London
www.learn2surf.co.za

Kagenuma Beach at Shonan, is a quick trip by train from Tokyo, which makes it popular with Japanese wanting to wash away the city stress. *Courtesy T-Stick*

Dolphin Bay Surf Tours
www.sunshine-coast.co.za

Durban, KwaZulu-Natal
South Beach
Learn 2 Surf—Durban
www.learn2surf.co.za

Roxy Surf School
www.roxysurfschool.co.za

SPAIN
Bilbao, Basque Country
Nomad Surfers Surfing Holildays—
Bilbao Surfcamp & Surfaris
www.nomadsurfers.com

Tapia, Leon, Castile, and Leon
Surfhouse—Tapia
www.surfhouse.org/html/surfhouse.html

Playa da Razo, Costa da Morte, Galicia
Surf & Rock
www.surfandrock.com

**Conil de la Frontera/El Palmar,
Costa de la Luz, Spain**
Oceano Surf School
www.surf-school-spain.com

El Palmar Surf School
www.elpalmarsurf.com

SRI LANKA
Arugam Bay
Surf 'N Sun Guest House
www.go-lanka.com/Arugam_Bay/surf_sun/
surf_sun_guesthouse_arugam.html

Broulee Learn to Surf School
www.brouleesurfschool.com.au

TAIWAN
Jin Shan
Kenting Surf Shop Surf School
www.kentingsurfshop.com.tw

Surfer Slang

SURFERS AND LANDLUBBERS are two people divided by a common language. To those not familiar with surfer speak, a common conversation between surfers stating ordinary things can sound like Martian. Study this glossary, and speak surfing.

Left: Famed surfer Miki Dora rides tandem, circa 1960s.
Right: Pretty much as the name describes it—getting some air. *Shutterstock*

Aerial: An advanced maneuver where a surfer with enough speed hits a section of wave and flies through the air, hopefully to land back on the wave and continue down the line.

Aggro: An Australian expression for aggressive surfing or an aggressive surfer.

Airdrop: When passing from the crest of a wave to the trough, sometimes a surfer will break contact with the wave entirely. This is not an aerial, but an airdrop. Sometimes it's intentional and sometimes it's fun—especially when you make it. Airdrops can also lead to bad wipeouts

All-time: A superlative to describe a day of waves or a single wave or a maneuver on a wave or anything related to surfing that is almost unprecedented in its singular greatness.

Aloha: A Hawaiian greeting that means "hello" or "goodbye."

Amped: Excited, energized.

Arvo: An Australian expression for "afternoon" that has crept into semi-general use in surfer slang.

Awesome: An expression of approval, often multiplied by the word "totally."

Back: The back of the wave. Some surfers measure wave height from the back of the wave. "Back" can also mean "outside" when you're Down Under, as in the Australian expression, "Out the back."

Backdoor: When taking off on a peak wave, good surfers will take off on the right side of the peak and drop in under the falling lip, going left. That is called "backdooring a wave."

Backwash: Wave energy that washes up the beach and returns to sea. When an incoming wave collides with backwash, the result can be fun or it can be a wipeout.

Baggies: A retro expression for surf trunks. Technically, baggies go below the knee.

Bail: An evasive maneuver, done in the face of danger. A surfer can bail his board when he is caught inside, bail off his board when he is about to get run over, or bail out in the face of a closed-out section by jumping off your board.

Ballistic: Doing something at a high level.

Banks: Aussie shorthand for "sand banks" or "sand bars."

Barrel: A late-twentieth-century expression for the **curl** or the **green room**. The hollow, breaking part of the wave.

Beef: To argue or physically fight. A Hawaiian pidgin expression.

Blow it: To make a mistake.

Boil: An area of unsettled water over shallow places in a reef or sandbar.

Bomb: A big wave. One that is bigger than the rest in a set or on a day of waves.

Bombing: When the waves are big and consistent. Synonyms: **going off**, **firing**, **smoking**.

Bonzer: A three-fin surfboard that became popular in the 1970s and 1980s and that was the precursor for the Thruster.

Aggro:

An Australian expression for aggressive surfing or an aggressive surfer.

Booger: A derogatory term for bodyboarders. Also: **doormat, gutslider, shark biscuit, speed-bump, sponger.**

Bottom: Can refer to the underside of a surfboard, or also the ocean floor. Also the trough of the wave, as in "bottom turn."

Bottom turn: The first turn on a wave, comes after takeoff and the drop, and before everything else. A bottom turn sets up the rest of the wave and determines many things.

Bowl: A part of the wave made hollow and steep by water depth. A wave can be a bowl at the beginning, or a bowl can appear at any part of a wave.

Bro: Surfers call each other this a lot. Brah is the Hawaiianization of bro.

Burn: Same meaning as **snake** or **drop in**. To burn someone on a wave is to break the accepted etiquette and ride in front of another surfer who has better position.

Bust: As in "bust a move." To perform something.

Carve: To do a particularly sharp turn. Surfers can "carve a bottom turn," or "carve an off the top" or "carve a cutback." To tell a surfer "You were really carving," is a compliment.

Caught inside: When a surfer is out of position and on the wrong side of a breaking wave, that is called getting "caught inside." Sometimes to escape a surfer will try to paddle over, under or through a breaking wave. Sometimes this works. Caught inside also means confronting rows of broken whitewater.

Cave: Another expression for **tube** or **barrel**. So-named because the area of a breaking wave sometimes resembles the interior of a cave.

Chandelier: Water falling in pieces at a barrel opening, threatening to bar the rider from exiting the tube.

Classic: A favored surfer adjective. Waves, days of surfing, surfing eras, surfboards, maneuvers, parties, girls, guys, jokes, situations can all be classic. And classic doesn't necessarily refer to the age of something.

Clean: A favorable condition, when wind and tides and currents conspire to keep the ocean surf smooth, and waves break evenly, with no sections.

Close out: When a wave or a section breaks all at once, it's "closing out."

Cloudbreak: A wave breaking well out to sea, almost on the horizon.

Cooking: A somewhat outmoded term for "good surf."

Coral head: Many of the world's most famous surf spots are formed by coral heads, including Teahupoo, Lance's Rights, and most of the surf spots in Polynesia and Indonesia. Coral heads and human skin do not mix.

Cover up: A tube ride that is less intense, similar to "locked in."

Cranking: Same meaning family as **going off, firing, pumping**: to describe when surf conditions come together to make quality, consistent surf.

Bust:

As in "bust a move." To perform something.

Cruise: To surf in a casual manner. Not aggressive.

Curtain: A poetic expression for the falling part of a wave, between the crest and the trough.

Cutback: A turn usually performed out on the "flats" or "shoulder" of the wave to redirect a surfer back to the curl, and where the energy is.

Da kine: A Hawaiian expression that generally means "good" but can mean many things.

Dawn patrol: To go surfing first thing in the morning, before the sun comes up. Some surfers love the dawn patrol, some don't. But it's a way to get out and get some waves before the crowd or contrary winds come up.

Deep/deeper: Deep refers to the vertical depth of water, but also to a surfer's position on a wave. The closer to the curl you are, the "deeper" you are. Skilled surfers can take off "deeper" on a wave than unskilled surfers.

Delam: Short for "delamination." A sort of ding, when the fiberglass and resin outer coating of a surfboard separates from the foam. This can be caused by sunlight, heat, or repeated pressure of a knee or body part against the surfboard.

Dialed: To understand something, or know how to do something well.

Ding: A hole or fracture in a surfboard. Usually dings are fixable, and there is an art to fixing dings.

Double up: When a larger wave overtakes a smaller wave sometimes they combine their energy into a "double up." A wave can double up on takeoff, or there can be a section down the line that doubles up. Double ups can lead to thrilling rides or bad wipeouts.

Down the line: A wave that is "down the line" is a walled-up wave, usually a point break, like Rincon, Puerto Rico or Jeffreys Bay, South Africa. Down the line also refers to sections of the wave that are coming up as a surf proceeds.

Draining: An expression that describes a hollow section of wave pulling all the water off a sandbar or reef.

Dodgy: An Australian term, similar to **sketchy** or **suss**. "We were going to paddle out at Gland on the low tide, but that one end section looked dodgy. So we gave it a miss and had jaffles for breakfast."

Drilled: Wiping out, or getting hit by a wave.

Drop: The start of a ride, off the peak.

Drop in: Two meanings. A surfer can "drop in" to a wave on takeoff. If another surfer takes off in front of that surfer, that is also a "drop in."

Duck dive: An advanced technique for using the energy of a breaking wave to get under and out the back and avoid taking that energy on your head.

Dump: When a wave breaks hard, all in one section, in a way that makes it unrideable.

Epic: A superlative to describe wave size and quality, parties, surfing ability, wipeouts. Just about everything.

Dialed:

To understand something, or know how to do something well.

Fade: Two meanings. On take off, a surfer will sometimes turn back into the meat of the wave. Also, "fading" is similar to dropping in.

Firing: Antonym to **cooking** or **going off**. When all the conditions come together, the surf is firing.

Flats: Not the steep part of a breaking wave. Also known as the **shoulder**.

Floater: A maneuver where a surfer uses speed and superb technique to go over the top of a crumbling section, and not around the bottom of it. Think: Kelly Slater.

Foam: Tiny bubbles massed together from the impact of the falling lip with the trough.

Foamball: Deep inside the tube, the foam that comes from the contact of the falling lip with the trough will cause a cushion of foam that pulses within the tube. The best surfers have learned to negotiate the foamball, either steering around it or using the energy to escape the tube.

Freefall: While riding a wave, when the board and the rails and the fin completely leave the surface of the water. Often happens on takeoff, or sometimes after a risky turn in a steep section of wave.

Free surfing: Riding waves for the fun of it, and not because one is in a contest, or being photographed, or doing it for anything other than pure enjoyment.

Frontside: A surfer facing a wave as they ride it. As opposed to backside.

Full on: Completely. As much as possible.

Gaff: A turn, similar to **hack**.

Glassy: A desirable ocean state where there is no wind and the ocean surface is smooth as glass.

Gnarly: A human or natural situation that is dangerous, risky, heavy.

Going off: When the swell is consistent and the tides are right and the winds are perfect.

Goofy foot: A surfer who rides with right foot forward and faces the wave going left.

Grommet: Australian expression for a young surfer, a derivative of **gremlin**. The shorter version is **grom**.

Gun: A big board for riding big waves.

Hack: An especially aggressive turn or maneuver.

Hang loose: A Hawaiian expression, usually accompanied by the **shaka** hand gesture, which espouses an easygoing, carefree philosophy.

Hang time: The amount of time a surfer spends in the air in the performance of an aerial maneuver.

Haole: Hawaiian term for "foreign," or "foreigner." **Haole** can be used to describe plants, animals, or people, but is often used derogatorily, in a nonwelcoming way.

Hawaiian scale: A way of measuring waves, different from the mainland scale or the Aussie scale. Hawaiians tend to underestimate wave size compared to other surfing cultures. A 6-foot (1.8-meter) wave on the Hawaiian scale is much larger than a 6-foot (1.8-meter) wave in California or France.

Going off:

When the swell is consistent and the tides are right and the winds are perfect.

Heat: A competitive period, that can range from 15 minutes to an hour.

Heavy: A qualitative superlative for a daring human act or a powerful, dangerous natural situation. A wave can be heavy, and a surfer's position on a wave can be heavy.

Hold down: A sometimes terrifying experience, where a wipeout is followed by a long period of turbulence under water. Hold downs will test a surfer's oxygen-burning capacity and sense of cool. The two-wave and three-wave hold down is something to be feared and avoided.

Hole: A deep part of a sandbar or reef.

Hollow: A wave that breaks hard and round over a shallow bottom is a hollow wave. Offshore winds, tides, and currents can also add to the hollowness of a wave.

Hot dog: Surfing a wave with a lot of showy maneuvers. "Hot dogging" is a somewhat antiquated expression that goes back to the 1960s. "A mature man will never remain a hotdogger," surfer Sam Reid said in 1966. But modern surfers still use hot dog to describe a lot of maneuvers on wave.

Hottie: A superlative term for a good surfer or an attractive member of the opposite sex.

Howzit?: An expression borrowed from Hawaiian pidgin, asking about the state of a person, place, or thing. "Howzit, brah, how's the surf?"

Impact zone: The area where waves are breaking and there is impact from the falling lip meeting the trough in swift collision and also a lot of disturbed water and foam.

In position: When a wave is approaching, there are good or bad places to be waiting for it. To be "in position" is also called "in the spot," which means you are deep enough to make the wave, but not too deep. The best position depends on the wave conditions and also the ability of the surfer.

Insane: A superlative describing an action, a condition, or a state of being.

Inside: The near-shore part of a surfbreak, where the waves are smaller and have less energy. Most surfers take off "outside" and ride the wave to the "inside."

Jacked/jacking: When a wave rears up suddenly and breaks hard and fast.

Kick out: A maneuver done at the end of a wave to exit it.

Konas: In Hawaii, the prevailing winds are the tradewinds that blow from northeast to southeast. Occasionally, southerly kona winds will blow across Hawaii, turning regular surf spots into slop and transforming usually sloppy spots into good waves. Outside Hawaii, dialed in surfers will refer to any contrary wind as konas.

Kook: An inexperienced or bad surfer.

Lacerate: Similar to **rip** or **shred**. An aggressive adjective describing what a hot surfer does to a wave.

Insane:
A superlative describing an action, a condition, or a state of being.

Landlord: An Australian term for shark. "Sometimes the landlord comes around to collect the rent."

Launch ramp: A section of wave that is perfect for boosting aerials or other radical maneuvers.

Ledge: Waves hitting the ocean bottom will sometimes have "ledge," which are wedges and other obstructions that move up the wave face, from the trough to the crest.

Lineup: The area of a surfbreak that is best for taking off. Some lineups are generally fixed, while other lineups shift with swell direction, currents, crowd, and the ability of the surfer.

Lip: The descending part of the curl of a breaking wave.

Lolo: Hawaiian word for "crazy."

Lull: The period of low energy in between sets of waves.

Mack: Big. "That day at Rincon was macking."

Mahalo: Hawaiian for "thank you."

Mental: Surfer speak for "crazy" or "radical."

Mini-gun: A surfboard roughly between 7 and 8 feet (2 to 2½ meters) long; larger than a standard shortboard, but smaller than a big-wave gun.

Mysto spot: A surf spot that breaks way out to sea, breaks only on certain swells, or breaks in an off-limit place.

North Shore: There are a lot of islands (and lakes) with shores on the north side, but in the surfing world, "North Shore" refers to the North Shore of Oahu—a "7-mile (11-kilometer) miracle" of some of the world's best waves for surfing.

Off its face: When the surf is really good.

Old school: Any surfboard, clothing style, surf style hair style, or other style that is more than 10 years older than the current style.

Onshores: Short for "onshore winds," which are usually contrary winds that deteriorate surf conditions—although some Waimea surfers like light onshores because the wave is easier to catch.

Outside: The part of the surf break that is the start of the lineup and beyond. Surfers will sometimes yell "Outside!" when a set is approaching.

Out the back: An Australian antonym for "outside," which has flowed into the mainstream of surfer speak.

Over the falls: To plummet from the crest of the wave to the trough, stuck in the lip of the wave.

Pearl: One facet of wiping out, in which the nose of a surfboard goes underwater. A shorter version of "pearl dive."

Penetrate: What a surfer hopes to do when they wipe out. "Penetrating" means making it under the water's surface, hopefully deep enough to avoid getting picked up by the wave and thrown over the falls.

Pipeline: One of the most famous surf spots in the world—a reef on the North Shore of Oahu that is considered a wave that must be mastered if a surfer is to be considered a master.

Pit: The impact zone of the wave, where the lip is descending to the trough, and the water is steep and pulled tight. Also known as the **Bowl**.

Over the falls:

To plummet from the crest of the wave to the trough, stuck in the lip of the wave.

Pitching: When the lip of a wave is throwing from the crest to the trough, it's pitching. Getting "pitched out" is what happens when a surfer gets stuck in the lip and goes over with it.

Pitted: To get deeply tubed.

Point break: A kind of wave that benefits from "refraction," where an incoming swell will feel shallow water at the top of a point and break, while the swell in deeper water moves along faster. Some of the world's best surf spots are point breaks: Noosa in Australia, Jeffreys Bay in South Africa, Rincon, and Malibu in California.

Prone out: A mostly antiquated term used by early big-wave surfers who didn't wear surf leashes, describing a situation where they would drop to their stomachs to ride out the foam when they couldn't make a wave or the wave closed out. Modern surfers will rely on their leashes for the most part, but there are still circumstances where a surfer will prone out—and then giggle when they use that antiquated term to describe their adventure.

Pull in: When a surfer commits to riding inside the tube, that surfer is "pulling in." This is not always a good idea, as some hollow waves offer no chance of escape. So pulling in is often a 50-50 commitment.

Pull off: To successfully do something.

Pumping: The condition when a swell is sweeping into a surf spot with consistent lines and it has power and quality.

Punt: To perform an aerial.

PWC: Personal Watercraft, also known as jet skis or water Harleys. There was a time when surfers and jet skiers just couldn't get along, but now PWC are used by tow surfers for catching big waves and for lifeguards and water patrols around the world.

Radical/rad: Perhaps the most common word in the surfer lexicon. Something that is rad is good, aggressive, risky, graceful, fast, critical.

Rash: Skin abrasions that can be caused by contact with surf wax, sand in surf wax, from rubbing against seams in wetsuits, or a reaction to materials in surf trunks.

Reef break: A wave that breaks over rock, coral, or some surface other than sand.

Re-entry: An increasingly retro term for turning up over a section and dropping back into the wave. Now known as a floater.

Re-form: When big waves break on an outer reef and the whitewater rolls in, sometimes that whitewater will feel shallow bottom and "re-form" into another wave. Re-form surfing on giant days is popular in Hawaii, because the energy is seemingly endless and you can ride a lot of waves.

Regular foot: A surfer who rides with their left foot forward, so they are facing the wave going right and riding backside going left.

Retro: Something that uses a fashion or style from a bygone era.

Rhino chaser: A retro but still cool term for a board for riding big waves.

Punt:

To perform an aerial.

Rideable: The antonym of "unsurfable." Rideable surf suggests bad quality, but there is still enough size or shape to offer fun or thrills.

Rip: Two meanings. To "rip a wave" is to ride aggressively and confidently and with style. Also, "rip" is short for "rip tide."

Rip tide: A current of water that has been pushed in by waves and is escaping through a channel, back out to sea. Rip tides can be dangerous and will drown you, but smart surfers will use rips for paddling in and out of the impact zone.

Rocker: The curve of a board from tail to nose, as seen from the side. Often when surfers refer to rocker, they are talking about the nose of the board and how it is elevated from the horizontal.

Rock up: An Australian expression that has entered the mainstream through the social intercourse of international surfing. To rock up means to arrive.

Rogue wave: Rogue waves are open ocean waves that are much bigger than the current sea state. They have been responsible for sinking or threatening ships from the *Edmund Fitzgerald* on the Great Lakes to the *Queen Elizabeth II* in the north Atlantic.

Rush: A physical state of often extreme well-being, inspired by adrenaline coursing up from the kidneys to the brain—usually caused by extreme acts.

Scratch: To paddle hard.

Section: A part of a wave that is determined by bottom contour, swell direction, wind, tides, currents, and other factors. A wave can "section" in front of a surfer, which means it breaks out of synch with the curl line.

Session: A period of time when you are surfing. Also known as a **sesh**.

Set: Waves arrive in groups, known as "sets." Some sets can have just one wave, others can have 20 or more. In general, the more waves in a set, the better, unless you are caught inside and about to drown.

Shacked: A modern 1990s expression for getting tubed.

Shaka: A Hawaiian hand gesture—similar to the Texas gesture for "Hook 'em, Horns!" except using the thumb and the pinkie—not the index finger and the pinkie. The shaka hand gesture can mean any number of things: Hello, goodbye, nice job, go away, or "Play 'Free Bird'!"

Shaper: Shorthand for "surfboard shaper," a species of human who perform great acts of functional craftsmanship, despite being overworked, underpaid, and constantly exposed to toxic materials.

Shifty: When waves are coming in from all angles and breaking in different places with no set lineup, surfers describe this as "shifty."

Shorebreak: When waves break directly on the shore, a few inches or feet (2.5 centimeters to 1 meter) from dry sand. Shorebreak waves generally have no shape and are not rideable.

Shred: To surf a wave aggressively.

Shut down: Similar to **close out**, when a section breaks in front of a surfer and ends a ride.

Shred:

To surf a wave aggressively.

Sick: A superlative that is a synonym to "very good."

Sideshore wind: When the wind is blowing at an angle into the waves—not offshore, which is good, or onshore, which is bad— then the winds are sideshore, which can sometimes be good and sometimes bad.

Single fin: Until the 1970s, almost all surfboards had only one fin. The **twin-fin** and the **Thruster** have made the single fin outmoded, for the most part, although some longboarders and shortboarders still prefer the one fin.

Skeg: An older expression for surfboard fin, but one that is still used.

Slab: A particularly heavy reefbreak coming out of deep water and breaking in very shallow water.

Slot: A good part of the wave, where the most energy is, or a line that gets you through a difficult part of the wave and out the other side.

Smoking: When surf conditions are optimum.

Snake: Can mean dropping in on another surfer, but snaking can also mean paddling around a surfer to get better position on a wave. Also known as **weaseling**.

Soup: Broken lines of white water are also called "soup," although this expression is not as popular as it used to be.

Spat out: When the compressed air inside of a tube explodes and takes a surfer with it, that surfer has been "spit out" or "spat out" of a wave.

Spit: All of the energy and foam and pressure inside of a breaking wave sometimes looks for a way to escape, and that escape is horizontally, out of the tube, toward the shoulder. This ejaculation of foam and water is called "spit."

Stall: To slow the speed of a surfboard, sometimes to set up for a noseride on an oncoming section, or let the tube catch up or to stay inside the tube longer.

Stance: How surfers position their feet on a surfboard. Hawaiians would sometimes ride with their feet parallel, in what they called **bully style**. But modern surfers are either regular foots or goofy foots.

Stick: A somewhat outmoded slang expression for surfboard. Also, to complete a maneuver.

Stoked: A feeling of elation, usually brought on by a day of good waves, but other things like love and family and accomplishment can inspire that feeling as well.

Stonefish: Of the many critters, flora, and fauna that a surfer can step on in the ocean, this one is best avoided.

Stringer: The wood or other material that runs down the center of a surfboard to give strength and flexibility to the foam. Most surfboards have one stringer, but some longboards have multiples.

Stuff: To ride in front of another surfer and place them in a bad position.

Styling: To do something with grace, smoothness, elegance. A surfer

Stuff:

To ride in front of another surfer and place them in a bad position.

can be styling in an old car, wearing styling clothes, and pull up to the beach with a styling chick (or dude), paddle out off the beach stylishly and style their way across waves. What constitutes "style" changes from year to year, era to era, day to day.

SUP: Stand up paddleboard. A new kind of surfing derived from the old ways of the Waikiki beach boys. SUPpers ride very long surfboards that float and use paddles to propel through the water.

Surfari: A combination of "surf" and "safari"—an older expression for taking a trip to find surf.

Surf rat: A young surfer, as they often look like drowned rats when they get out of the water.

Sweet: An adjective of approval.

Swinging wide: Sometimes waves that have been breaking all in the same place will move to a different part of the reef. These waves are sometimes called "swingers."

Takeoff: The start of the wave.

Tandem: When two people ride on a surfboard at the same time.

Tear: To aggressively surf a wave.

Tombstone: When a surfer wipes out and is held under and his surfboard is on the surface, and the surfer and the board are still connected, the board is often pulled tail down, with the nose in the air. This is called "tombstoning," and suggests what is happening to the surfer below.

Tow surfing: A recent innovation that goes back to the early 1990s, where surfers use personal watercraft to tow into waves that are too big or gnarly to be caught under human power.

Tradewinds: Winds blowing from the tropical latitudes toward the equator blow in a regular pattern from east to west because of the spinning of the earth. In Hawaii, the trades blow from northeast to southwest, and these regular winds blow well over some famous surf spots—and are part of the reason these spots are famous.

Tri-fin: A surfboard with one center-fin, and two side fins. Also known as a **Thruster**.

Twin-fin: A surfboard design that goes back to the 1940s, but was popularized by Mark Richards and others in the 1970s and 1980s.

Walled up: When waves are breaking too fast and close to all at once, they are still rideable, but "walled up."

Water patrol: During surf contests and sometimes during free surf sessions, the water patrol are lifeguards and other trained professionals who make sure surfers behave themselves and are also on hand to rescue in case of emergencies.

Wedge: When backwash energy comes off the beach or a protuberance like a jetty and that backwash hits an incoming wave, the energies combine to form a "wedge" wave.

Wettie: Slang term for wetsuit.

Wipeout: The unsuccessful discompletion of a wave. Wipeouts have many shapes and flavors and can happen from taking off at the peak to kicking out at the end—and anywhere in between.

Walled up:

When waves are breaking too fast and close to all at once, they are still rideable, but "walled up."

About the Author

BEN MARCUS is the guy your mother warned you about. He grew up skateboarding and surfing in Santa Cruz, California, in the 1970s, during a time when everyone wore puka shells and O'Neill Supersuits or Animal Skins, had long blond hair, and rocked out to Honk, Blind Faith, and Jimi Hendrix. An era like that will hook anyone on surfing for life, and Ben was a stoked gremmie, surfing the east side of Santa Cruz at Pleasure Point and also the Santa Cruz Yacht Harbor and Rivermouth in the winter.

After graduating from high school, Ben traveled the world in search of the perfect wave. In the 1980s, he wrote a short story about a surfing adventure on the Spanish Basque coast and submitted it to *Surfer* magazine. *Surfer* hired him as associate editor, where he remained for ten years, writing about many of the changes in surfing—the discovery of Maverick's, the debut of tow surfing, the arrival of the New School, and stars such as Lisa Andersen, Kelly Slater, and Laird Hamilton.

Now here in the twenty-first century, Ben still surfs and travels as much as possible, writing for the *Surfer's Journal* and other publications. He's the author of Voyageur's *Surfing USA!*, *The Surfboard*, and *Surfing & the Meaning of Life*, as well as several other books for other publishers.

A portrait of the author as a young surfer dog, Malibu, California, 1970s.

MAY 29 2015

CPSIA information can be obtained at www.ICGtesting.com
Printed in the USA
LVOW02s0442220114

370322LV00009B/11/P

9 780760 336922